Fairy Tales and Art
Mirrored in Modern Consciousness

Fairy Tales and Art
Mirrored in Modern Consciousness

Monica Gold

Published by:
The Association of Waldorf Schools
of North America
Publications Office
38 Main Street
Chatham, New York 12037

Title: *Fairy Tales and Art Mirrored in Modern Consciousness*
Author: Monica Gold
Editor: David Mitchell
Copy Editor and Proofreader: Ann Erwin
Copyright permissions were obtained by the author, who holds all legal responsibility for them.
Cover Illustration: *Saint Michael the Archangel*, Luca Giordano
© 2012 by AWSNA Publications and Monica Gold
ISBN # 978-1-936367-27-6

Printed in China

*This book is dedicated to
my children and grandchildren.*

Mariah
Monica Gold

Contents

Thanks

I would like to thank Marina Matchavariani in the Republic of Georgia for her steadfast guidance during a long process of research which helped to clarify my ideas.

I also wish to thank Anthony Perzel for his skills in editing and photography. I gratefully appreciate his warm interest throughout the writing of this book.

I want to recognize Jeanne Lister for her suggestions regarding the subtleties of the English language, Marijn Eterman for the layout, and Celina Gold and Rita Taylor for a final reading.

A very special thanks goes to my husband, Andrew, and my daughters, Fiona, Celina, and Nadja, for their encouragement and the use of their childhood drawings.

Thank you also to all those who have shown an interest in this book and helped me along the way.

– Monica Gold
2011

Foreword

Occasionally we are reminded by the media of the youth demonstrations that took place in the 1960s when politicians, athletes, artists, members of the business community and many others attempted to express the thoughts and longings of that generation.

At that time, one idea uniquely found its way into speeches and print. It appeared on the walls of the Sorbonne University in Paris, well-known for its cultural heritage: *L'imagination au pouvoir*—'Let imagination reign!' In this case, the word *imagination* brought into play opportunities to revitalize social structures. It represented dynamic activism and it represented the future, but at that time many of those opportunities were lost. Yet, there were some who continued to work towards cultivating a lively imagination in order to enliven and bring about social change. Only living imagination can affect true change.

The author of this unique book, which represents the maturation of lifelong studies in philosophy and art, is one of these persons. Monica Gold, a mother, teacher, and engaged international social artist, found that by experiencing genuine fairy tales in the context of her understanding of anthroposophy, she was constantly inspired in her multifaceted international work.

Every reader who approaches this book with both head and heart will find it a constant source of living imagination, and in this way a fount of wisdom and strength. Wisdom is presented through intimated spiritual connections, and strength results from an inner intuitive understanding of the many illustrations. It is my hope that this book may find many avid readers.

– Mario Betti
2009

Introduction

The picture of a storytelling grandmother in a long skirt with a scarf around her shoulders, while children listen attentively at her feet, enthralled at hearing about princes and princesses, is an image of the past—or is it not? Today, when fairy tales are shared, they are mostly read from a book, and the magic that lived in the souls of the elderly as they stirred the children's imagination, is rarely found.

At the other end of the spectrum changes have also taken place in today's babies. Eyes that looked at us from the crib thirty years ago were dreamy; today babies seem ready to interact very soon after birth, and young children simply cannot wait to grow up. It has been my experience that they want to be met with an increased awareness for their needs. One such need is fulfilled when children listen to "old" fairy tales told by adults who carry the consciousness of the individual fairy tale in their hearts.

At the core of every fairy tale is a main character, portrayed amidst others, who stands for soul qualities and capabilities. These characteristics of the soul are represented as people and animals, real or mythical. Furthermore, these qualities live in every human being.

He who can penetrate the veil of the pictures sees the wicked witch, the fierce wolf, the beautiful princess and the handsome prince in a new and different light. The fairy tale ceases to be simply a form of entertainment; instead its characters become real and play a part in our life and in our soul development. This is so because true fairy tales rely on archetypes, and archetypes are inspired by the spiritual world; they are not fantasies. Children who hear fairy tales are closer to their angels than those who do not.

If humanity is on a path of evolution, which is clearly the case as will be readily seen through these pages, and if one can accept the discussion of the series of art pictures shown in the first chapter, then there must be a future goal for humanity. Such a goal has to do with a major change in human consciousness. It must take into account the existence of a spiritual world and a healthy social relationship between human beings, as well as an increased awareness for the well-being of our planet.

This book is an attempt to provide the thoughts and resource material necessary to foster an increased awareness of the world in which we live and a better understanding of the world of the fairy tale.

– Monica Gold
West Vancouver, 2011

Notes: If there is no date in an illustration tag, it could not be found. The author's use of the words man *or* mankind *and* he *or* him *applies to both the male and female genders. Sometimes* Prince, Princess *and* Father *are capitalized because the Prince stands as an image for humanity, the Princess as the higher self and the Father as God.*

Hunters
Mesolithic wall painting, Castellon, Spain

1 Little Red Riding Hood

Responsibility without love makes us inconsiderate.
Power without love makes us cruel.
Belief without love makes us fanatics.
Intelligence without love makes us dishonest.
–Lao Tse

In this day and age mankind still lives with an unfulfilled task. This task is to create a social setting with love. To see love working in a selfless way is, in spite of all other advances of our modern society, the only possibility for humanity's future.

However, this high ideal has always existed as a guide for humanity in fairy tales, where time and again we can imagine the force of love motivating a young Prince to strive toward his ultimate goal—that of winning the hand of a Princess—but only on the condition that he first face the task of transforming his inner self. In a fairy tale the Prince reaches his goal by overcoming the obstacles that he encounters while on his journey along a path. As he grows ever wiser, he awakens to his true feelings, develops clarity of thinking, and strengthens his resolve and will. The Prince's final reward, often after a long struggle, is marriage to the Princess. A fairy tale has the potential to cast a light on the human soul's higher character traits such as humility, devotion, selflessness, hope, faith, and goodness. These human qualities are woven metaphorically into the fairy tale. It is the reality of life that, as a greater number of human beings develop such qualities in full consciousness, humanity will venture closer to reaching its ideal, imbuing social life with love.

Our children hold the future of the planet Earth in their hands. We must consider carefully the seeds of guidance that we choose to offer them for their balanced growth and well-being. The world of the fairy tale is one such wondrous seed. In the fairy tale, mankind's path of evolution—with all its joys, trials, and tribulations essential for individual soul development—is depicted through creative imagination. It is extremely important that fairy tales remain pure, and they will continue to remain so as long as their originality is not tampered with through the use of subjective fantasy and intellectual modifications. Sadly, some fairy tales have been altered and even distorted simply because their original meaning and intent is no longer understood.

Fairy tales originate in a world invisible to the human eye, a world that can no longer be felt intuitively, as was the case in earlier times. Their subtle wisdom, perceived through the forces of the heart, is not readily available to modern intellectual thinking and has become more and more veiled. One can safely say that such wisdom cannot be grasped by intellect alone, yet many people today are earnestly interested in and seek to understand the hidden meanings in fairy tales.

There are different means by which a reader can connect to the imagination of a fairy tale. Life experience is certainly one of them. Another is through anthroposophy,[1] a modern science of the spirit that can shed light on the spiritual truths hidden in a fairy tale. Great works of art throughout the ages can also reveal those truths. Artists often manifest spiritual truths intuitively, and their creative expression becomes a powerful testimony of the time in which they live. Through their works of art they reveal the story of man's path of evolution.

In order to understand more clearly what a fairy tale may reveal, in the chapters that follow I will attempt to open the book of fairy tale imaginations and compare it to paintings and sculptures from the world of art. The stories will illuminate the path of mankind's evolution and show wherever possible how this evolution parallels the growth processes of a child. The reader needs to be conscious of the fact that truths hidden in an old fairy tale can be viewed from different angles, just as the facets of a diamond can be viewed from various sides. However, one thing is certain: With regard to true imagination, there is no place for fabrication or intellectualism.

In earlier days the storyteller would begin with "Once upon a time…" and end with "…and if they have not died, they are still alive today." These two expressions which form the opening and closing of the fairy tale are open-ended. They transport us into a world without beginning or end and represent eternity. One is tempted to argue that everything has a beginning and an end. Every day has a beginning and an end, and every year has a beginning and an end. Every life starts with birth and ends with death. And yet the reader is asked to accept the fact that a fairy tale has neither a beginning nor an end.

A fairy tale, if it is based on truth, transcends time. It connects us to a world of truths and laws which provide the basis for all that happens in the human soul, the world of nature, and the cosmos. In earlier times, people were intuitively aware of the universe. Their lives were directed by the rhythms and laws of the cosmos, which were accepted without question. These rhythms and laws had their foundation in spiritual realities and, although not directly perceptible, they continue to guide mankind even today.

In time, the doors that provided mankind with a direct connection to the spiritual world slowly began to close. Today however, through the writings, lectures, and insights of Rudolf Steiner,[2] one of the great initiates of the twentieth century, humanity is brought closer to a new conscious understanding of the spiritual world and a reconnection with spiritual laws that penetrate the universe, man, and nature.

In our time, most people live with vague abstractions regarding questions of man's origin. They are not aware of how profoundly man's well-being and health depend on spiritual laws and how important it is that he live in harmony with the cosmos. It is the aim of this book to show that the human being exists in the spiritual world as well as in the physical world.

1
Drawing by a nine-year-old child

Research has shown that a house drawn by a child generally refers to his or her own physical body.[3] When human beings incarnate into the physical, they have no memory of the spiritual world, although as young children they are still connected with it. This can be discovered in their drawings. It becomes apparent in illustration 1, drawn by a nine-year-old boy. On the one hand, he is obviously on earth, as he has drawn a house, trees, and a tricycle, while on the other, we can observe that much of his drawing is actively concentrated on the roof. This is so, because for him life continues, at least partly, in a world invisible to us. The heavy black roof line indicates the separation between the earthly as we know it and a heavenly world.

Long ago, when man still felt united with his spiritual origins, he did not need religion. When man entered the age of Kali Yuga, a time when he was no longer able to look into the spiritual world, he was given religion.[4] In Latin, *religare* means 'to reconnect.' Religion is needed as long as the door to the spiritual world is closed. In the future, when man's consciousness will include the world of the spirit, he will experience a different reality. Human evolution is the process of man's separation from a unity with his spiritual origin and his eventual return to it.

Such spiritual facts can be found mirrored in fairy tales, and this depiction can help human beings reconnect with the supersensible world. This is why true fairy tales are strengthening, harmonizing, and life-giving for every child and adult who comes into contact with them. When children incarnate, they bring with them trust and faith that there is goodness, truth, and love awaiting them. These qualities are retained throughout their early years unless they run into opposite experiences.

2
Hunters
Mesolithic wall painting, 15,000–10,000 BC
Castellon, Spain

4
Ombra
Etruscan, Etruscan Museum
Volterra, Italy

5
Elongated Figurine
Etruscan
End of 5th c. BC
Umbria, Italy

3
Wounded Man and Rhinoceros
assumed earliest Upper
Palaeolithic 10,000 BC,
Lascaux, Dordogne, France

Human Evolution Mirrored in Works of Art

We will now journey together through the world of art. Man's path through evolution is interwoven with his creative abilities. The following sculptures, paintings, and drawings will show in a simple way how the human being has perceived himself throughout the ages. The earliest testimonies of human beings representing themselves in drawings come from the Castellon wall paintings in Spain, about 10,000 BC (illustration 2). Many questions arise concerning the hunters and much can be learned while one searches for answers. For example, how important are the hunters' heads, hands, and feet to the artist? How important are their spears? What is it that lives most strongly in these drawings? Is it not their elongated bodies, their movement? Was man floating more than walking in that distant past? How incarnated into his body was he?

In the Lascaux cave painting *Wounded Man and Rhinoceros* (illustration 3), the artist experiences the strength and power of the bull's force. Indeed, the drawing looks more like a bull than a rhinoceros. The artist does not draw attention to the head of the animal nor to that of the little man; instead the artist points to the bull's capability of reproduction. The human being looks quite helpless and overcome by these forces of nature—he does not yet stand upright. People of that time heard the voices of the spirit, speaking through the wind. Thunder and lightning caused fear of unknown gods. They still perceived the workings of a spirit world.

The Etruscan figures in illustrations 4 and 5 were created around 500 BC, approximately 9500 years after the Castellon wall painting of the hunters. The figures are no longer floating or in movement. Man now experiences himself upright with an elongated body and a tiny head. It seems as if his head is in the clouds. These figures show us that the human being is still in the process of arriving on the earth. While the Etruscan is surrounded by the gifts of the earth—stones, flowers and animals—he is still unaware of them; whereas later the Greek, for example, perceived himself as an organic part of his natural surroundings which were filled with spirit and elemental beings. Nature was alive for him.

Later, approximately AD 140, one finds the Roman sculpture of Antinous, a friend of Emperor Hadrian. He is posing as Bacchus (illustration 6). What is important for our theme is that man is now looking at his world objectively. He is consciously making use of the fruit of the earth.

Around the year AD 1500, at the time of the Renaissance, Raphael painted *The Three Graces* (illustration 7). While the Etruscan figures show that man was not conscious of his connection to the physical body, Raphael's figures are drawn with intense vitality, serenity, and a feeling for space. This painting offers us the possibility of absolute balance and harmony. Here the human beings, represented by the Three Graces, are completely in tune with their physical bodies and harmony.

Another important step is shown in Alessandro Allori's drawing *The Flayed* (illustration 8). The representation of the human figure is no longer solved by mere accuracy of hand and eye. "It was brought into due relation with geometry and mathematics, and then with scientific anatomy. The principles of art became, in consequence, a matter of precise and demonstrable knowledge that could in some measure be acquired by study, and used as a firm basis for the employment of natural gifts."[5] In other words, man began to use his intellect, which led to a separation of subject and object, i.e., man and his surroundings. With his developing intellect, man himself became an object for analysis.

6
Statue of Antinous as a God
Roman, AD 140

7
The Three Graces
Raphael
(1483–1520)

8
The Flayed
Alessandro Allori
(1535–1607)

9
The Three Bathers
Pierre-Auguste Renoir
(1841–1919)

It may be said that while Raphael was painting *The Three Graces* out of his heart forces, the intellect appeared in the presentation by Alessandro Allori. In *The Three Bathers* (illustration 9), painted by Pierre-Auguste Renoir in 1882, beauty and the beginnings of sensuousness are added to the balanced composition. Playful and delightfully innocent, the girls bring us a step closer to the world in which we now live.

With Picasso's *Nude in the Forest* (illustration 10, next page), the body as it appears to our physical eye is no longer of interest. The world of art grapples with an intellectual understanding of the human figure. What matters in Cubist painting is the carefully constructed form. Man becomes a lifeless object. Dark and light colors, triangles, and squares appear as if cast in stone.

10
Nude in the Forest
Pablo Picasso
(1881–1973)

11
Woman I
Willem de Kooning
(1904–1997)

Now let us consider Willem de Kooning's *Woman I* (illustration 11). The human being is no longer seen as beautiful. Instead, chaos and destruction reign. Upon encountering such a painting, one can ask the following questions: What is the artist trying to show? Does he see the human being in a struggle with good and evil forces? Finally we take a look at the Spanish painter Joan Miró's *Self-Portrait* (illustration 12), which reveals a modern human being's perception of himself. Thus the history of art reflects how man's perception of himself has changed. In our time, the spiritual world has largely been forgotten because our spiritual eyes and ears are closed.

Very slowly man has evolved and has become more conscious of the earth and of his immediate surroundings. Rudolf Steiner said:

> We cast our gaze back to remote times and found that men did not issue from a merely animalistic stage of development, but from a form in which they possessed the power of clairvoyance as a congenital endowment. People of that time were clairvoyant, even though their consciousness still lacked the ability to say "I am." The capacity for self-consciousness was something they had to acquire gradually, and for this they had to forfeit their old clairvoyance. In the future the time will come again when all men will be clairvoyant, but without loss of self-consciousness, the "I am."[6]

12
Self-Portrait
Joan Miró
(1893–1983)

The history of art clearly shows humanity's separation from the spiritual world. The closing of the doors to that world and the subsequent development of the intellect have resulted in a predominantly intellectual view of who we are and of our world. The journey to a reconnection with our spiritual origin is not easy. It is fraught with temptations, dangers, and hardships. A creative picture of this journey is found in the simple and well-known fairy tale that follows.

Little Red Riding Hood

Once upon a time, a young girl lived with her mother in a house in the country. One day, her grandmother gave her a red cap. It suited her so well that everybody called her Little Red Riding Hood.

When her grandmother became ill, her mother sent Little Red Riding Hood to visit her. She gave her a basket with a loaf of bread and a bottle of wine, warning her not to leave the path. The old woman lived in a cottage in the center of the forest.

Little Red Riding Hood set out on her journey. On her way, she came to a meadow covered with flowers. There she met a big wolf. The wolf said to her, "Look at all these flowers. Pick them and take them to your grandmother." Little Red Riding Hood was delighted with his suggestion and ran from one flower to another until her arms could no longer hold all the beautiful flowers.

In the meantime, the wolf ran to the grandmother's cottage and, after he entered her room, swallowed her in one gulp. He fastened her lace cap on his head, slipped into her bed and waited for Little Red Riding Hood to arrive. When she finally came to the door, he asked her to come into the room. She, however, did not recognize her grandmother and was puzzled by her ears, eyes, nose, and mouth.

"Why do you have such big ears, Grandmother?" she asked timidly.

"So that I can hear you better!" answered the wolf.

"Why then, Grandmother, do you have such big eyes?"

"So that I can see you better!"

"Why do you have such a big nose, Grandmother?"

"So that I can smell you better!" he replied.

"Grandmother, why do you have such a terribly big mouth?" With this question the wolf jumped out of bed and swallowed up Little Red Riding Hood. Then he went back to bed and snored loudly.

The forester happened to be passing by and heard the noise. "That does not sound like the grandmother," he thought. "I had better have a look inside the cottage!" When he saw the wolf in bed, he immediately knew what had happened, took out his large scissors and cut open the wolf's stomach.

First the grandmother came out and then out jumped Little Red Riding Hood. Together they collected stones and put them into the wolf's stomach, sewed him up and celebrated their reunion with the bread and wine which Little Red Riding Hood had brought. Later, when the wolf woke up, he felt thirsty, went to the well, and because he was so heavy, he fell into its depths and drowned.

Children's Creative Drawings Recall the Past

One of the questions raised frequently in our time is, "Aren't fairy tales too cruel for children?" The wolf swallows first the grandmother and then the little girl. It is, after all, Little Red Riding Hood with whom a young listener would identify most.

During a discussion amongst adults, a child overhearing their concerns came to his mother saying: "Mummy, your wolf is not the same as mine!"

If one remembers the path of the slowly incarnating human being throughout the centuries, as was shown by the representations of artistic works, it will be interesting to have a brief look at drawings done by children, which portray their inner experiences. It is natural that the content of a child's drawing changes as he or she matures. In illustrations 13, 14, and 15 it becomes apparent that the path travelled by humanity over an extensive period of time is repeated, though briefly, by each incarnating human being. A young child feels just as connected to nature and the spirit as humanity felt in ancient times.

The children's illustrations definitely remind the viewer of the old Etruscan sculptures. The person portrayed in illustration 13 appears to be floating in the air and the light orange color radiates life, while the gesture portrays a gentle caring. This drawing suggests harmony. Could the young artist have been drawing an angel looking down at the earth?

In a drawing by a five-year-old Russian child (illustration 14), one is reminded of the Etruscan figures in illustrations 4 and 5.

Since young children do not yet live in their intellect, they intuitively grasp the truths of the fairy tale, just like mankind did in the past. Does illustration 15 show a child in the forest protected by trees as once humanity was protected by higher beings?

13

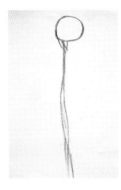

14

15

Three drawings by young children

Children's Creative Drawings and Paintings Reveal Truths

There is an urgent need for the realization that time is required for a child to incarnate. A deep understanding by parents and teachers of a child's development will help the child's body and soul unfold harmoniously. The method by which adults apply this understanding will also determine the child's inner sense of security when he is older. In relation to this, the anthroposophical physician Wolff Husemann says, "The small child perceives and experiences his environment as an extension of his own body. If the surroundings are sound and beautiful and if true thoughts are thought in them, then health-giving forces flow through the child: He thrives and attains his proper state of development. If his environment is permeated by malignant influences, by hatefulness and false thoughts, then the child's further development is seriously hampered or altogether blocked in important ways, as in many institutionalized children."[7]

The last two illustrations show drawings by an eight-year-old boy (illustration 16), and a seven-year-old girl (illustration 17). The boy was born prematurely. Consider the strength of the tree and the interest in all that is connected to the environment: the rainbow, the sun and moon, the star and the cloud from which it begins to rain. The drawing is complete and beautiful in its

16

17

composition. The sun is so real to him; it has a face, while he himself does not. When one looks at the child in the drawing, he seems to hardly touch the earth. The artist, although knowledgeable of the spheres around him, is not yet conscious of his own hands and feet. The arms are drawn from the neck area and they are very light yellow, the basket is floating on air, and the general colors are bright. There is, of course, a difference in drawings between boys and girls, but the boy's drawing shows clearly that he still has his home in a world of spirits.

Such a child needs special consideration in his upbringing since too much intellectual information might affect his physical and emotional health. The beautiful drawing of the seven-year-old girl is easily understood. Consider the solid way in which she stands on the earth and her charming interaction with the animals. Rhythm and visual perspective dominate the scene.

Between the ages of five and eight, a child begins to be absorbed by all the fairy tale images of princes and princesses. This is also the time when children subconsciously long to feel the truths or wisdom that live in them, because it allows a connection with the spiritual world from which he or she has come. As was said, a child perceives the truth on another level and does not require the interpretations of fairy tales. Indeed, that would be wrong. This connection can be enhanced through an adult who tells the fairy tales, knowing what lives in them rather than reading them aloud from a book. Saying prayers with and for the child before sleep can also be helpful. All of this can be imbued with a special atmosphere of candlelight.

Mankind Is Free to Choose between Good and Evil

Returning to the story of *Little Red Riding Hood*, we may ask what the wisdom-filled imaginations of the tale can reveal to the questioning mind. After all, the main character concerns all of us because she stands before us as a representative of humanity. The answer to this question will be clear if one considers the teachings of Spiritual Science. From those teachings it is known that in the past the whole of humanity lived like a child of God, protected and guided by a spiritual world. In accordance with Eastern tradition, Rudolf Steiner calls the time from 3100 BC to AD 1899, the age of Kali Yuga, meaning The Dark Age.[8] During these five thousand years, man slowly separated from the benevolent spiritual world so that he could become a free human being consciously living on the earth with all its temptations and wonders. Humanity's interest in earthly matters has become ever more important, as was shown through the pictures and sculptures—the history of art that traces man's path of descent.

In other words, as long as humanity was protected and nurtured by the divine world and remained dependent on the source of its origin, man was unable to become an independent and free individual. Simply stated, man's task is to develop the strength with which to resist the counter-forces of evil that he meets daily, and at the same time to become a loving soul in the service of mankind. Keeping these indications in mind, what follows is a possible interpretation of the characters in the story of *Little Red Riding Hood*.

In the fairy tale, the old and wise grandmother may be seen as man's link to his spiritual origin. The fact that man was in the process of evolving, slowly separating and becoming estranged from his divine origin, is expressed by a symbolic red hood. The hood was given to the young girl by her grandmother, not by her mother or a friend. A hood separates us from the sky. This could perhaps indicate that influences coming from the spiritual world can no longer easily reach the human being.

The wolf can be seen as the representation of evil. It is evil that tempts the girl to pick the beautiful, colored flowers, enticing her to forget her duty to take the bread and wine to her grandmother. She follows only her longing to pick more and more flowers, a metaphor for the pursuit of earthly pleasures. When she finally finds her path back to her grandmother's house, having been swayed by the pleasures of life, she has to bear the consequence of having strayed from the path—she is swallowed by the wolf!

It is, of course, human nature to follow the temptations that are placed in man's way, but these temptations have the potential of slowly making humanity unhappy and eventually even destroying the earth. Man was made in the image of God as stated in the Bible,[9] but the human being has estranged himself from the perfect image through the Fall and has to regain it anew. The return journey, as described in fairy tales, is a path involving struggles and temptations.

While the wolf lies in bed snoring, having swallowed Little Red Riding Hood, it is the forester who discovers the tragedy. The forester in this story is a metaphor for an initiate, someone who knows his way in the darkness of the forest. Through clairvoyant insight, he sees what other people cannot see. Initiates are human beings who have, through their own striving and purification, developed capacities of spiritual seeing and hearing. In this story it is the forester alone who can create order and bring to light the evil doings of the wolf.

As was noted previously, a child intuitively feels the spiritual value of such a story where good overcomes evil and is strengthened morally, rather than being frightened and intimidated. But if the parent fears for the child, that fear will be picked up by the child.

According to Spiritual Science, the divine plan for our planet Earth is to evolve into a planet of love, a future stage of spiritual maturity which human beings will eventually acquire. Rudolf Steiner pointed out that "when the Earth has reached the end of its evolution, love should permeate it through and through. Let us understand clearly what is meant by the expression: the Earth is the planetary life condition for the evolution of love. …What then is essential for love? …It is that he is in full possession of his self-consciousness, that he be fully independent. …To this end the human being had to become an ego being."[10]

This is the reason that counterforces were placed as impediments on our path of evolution. These forces tempt us with all the desires and possibilities the earth has to offer, saying: "Enjoy everything, don't be concerned about a spiritual path, just live and be happy." Mankind now has the opportunity to realize his spiritual origin and may seek the path back to the spiritual world in total freedom.

Spiritual insight opens only through patient work and purification, while the sole pursuit of happiness and pleasures hinders the process of evolution. Little Red Riding Hood tried it and was swallowed by the wolf. Instead of continuing on to her grandmother's house, her true destination, she listens to the wolf who diverts her, and for that she has to pay the price.

The grandmother represents the divine while Little Red Riding Hood is symbolic of mankind. Both are swallowed by the wolf, a representation of evil forces. When Little Red Riding Hood arrives at her grandmother's cottage, it is the wolf, an animal, that awaits her. Is this not a beautiful example of Darwinism? The idea of man's evolving from animals continues to hinder our potential for understanding our true spiritual origin, leaving it hidden.

Finally, the fairy tale concludes with the forester. As the initiate, he exposes the evil wolf, which disappears down into the well, and restores the grandmother and Little Red Riding Hood to life. This is celebrated through the partaking of bread and wine. The Christian symbols of bread and wine have been regarded as important for the path back to man's origin. One may well ask why. In the Old Testament when Melchizedek meets his divine guest, he serves bread and wine. At the Last Supper, Christ showed a way of connecting Himself to mankind through the sacraments of bread and wine.

It became a new possibility for mankind's spiritual development and a reconnection with God, our divine origin, out of freedom and love. This process in theology is called *theosis*. Until such a journey is undertaken, religion, mythology, fairy tales, and world literature are needed to help mankind remain connected to the spiritual world, a world of living truths.

In this first chapter, an attempt was made to show, through works of art, how man lived in ancient times, protected by the spiritual world. Like a young child, unaware of himself, he slowly developed into an independent being.

The fairy tale *Little Red Riding Hood* tells the story of man's confrontation with evil on the path towards freedom. However, his story is not yet complete, for it is out of his newly-won freedom that he will have to reconnect himself with the hierarchical world and recognize that he was truly made in the image of God.

> While becoming an Ego,
> The human being
> Had to free himself long ago
> From the reality of spirit
> And, dying, dive deep
> Into the dark abysses of existence,
> There to kindle in the shadowy depths,
> Through struggle
> With the opposing might of death, the strength of the human I.
> As being of light he now ascends into the bright shining of the spirit,
> Thus binding anew
> The depths with the heights.[11]
>
> – Gerhard Reisch, artist

Angel
Duccio di Buoninsegna

2 The Little Golden Box

The reader of a fairy tale can experience a very exciting moment when he becomes conscious of its creative imagery. Fairy tales are filled with wisdom and truths, to which modern man has little or no direct access, as will become apparent in the chapters that follow.

When one sees, hears, or occupies oneself with great works of art and listens, for example, to Beethoven's *Fifth Symphony*, or looks at a Raphael painting such as *The Sistine Madonna*, one feels warmed and enlivened, perhaps even joyful! In the same way, when a fairy tale is told to a child between the ages of four and seven or eight and when the adult in the telling is able to connect to the truths that live in the fairy tale, the child also inwardly rejoices in a very special way. The adult is then able to carry a precious unseen gift to the child, which works deeply into the child's whole being.

In order to understand what lives in a fairy tale, the story needs to be looked at in detail. For some readers this might seem difficult. However, due to our intellectual modern mind, it is a necessity of our time to connect with the true meaning of a fairy tale, in order that its original intention is preserved. Furthermore, when the adult is able to embrace some of the mysteries spoken about in the fairy tale, there may arise in his or her own soul feelings of reverence and wonder. These feelings are then intuitively felt by the child. This becomes nourishment for the Angel Being who is able to help the child.

The Reality of Angels

Since angels are not visible to the human eye, how can a modern human being become convinced of their reality? Even if one is open-minded, questions may remain. At one time, I was also unsure about the existence of angels, and I would like to share an experience which opened a new perception for me.

I was listening to a lecture on fairy tales, where the speaker was discussing the content of *Little Red Riding Hood*. The imaginations represented by the grandmother, the little girl, the wolf, and the forester were explained in detail, and my thoughts found their way into many new discoveries. Since the story was a favorite of mine, it was also well-known to our six-year-old daughter. A few days following the lecture, when I told her the fairy tale with the newly acquired wisdom living in my soul, she seemed more attentive than usual. At the end she gave me the biggest embrace and said, "This was the best story that you have ever told me! I have never heard it before!" She did not let me out of her sight for two days. It was as if a new bond had been formed. I believe that

18
*Pharaoh Chephren
with the Horus Falcon*
ca. 2700 BC
Egypt

through her angel, she had grasped intuitively the underlying truths of the fairy tale. Of course I had not shared its deeper wisdom with her directly; that wisdom she experienced in her subconscious, where it remained. I did wonder, however, whether children have an invisible little bird sitting on their shoulders, like the Egyptian sculpture, *Pharaoh Chephren with the Horus Falcon* (illustration 18). The falcon in this case represents a connection to the spiritual world and perhaps even indicates divine inspiration.

The word 'inspiration' comes from the Latin *inspirare* 'to breathe in.' This sculpture shows that through the falcon Horus, the Pharaoh is connected to truths coming from higher realms, giving him the wisdom to guide his people. Who is it that inspires the human being from higher spheres? In a lecture on the Gospel of St. Mark, Rudolf Steiner said: "In the epoch of post-Atlantean culture preceding our own, men were still endowed, to some extent, with faculties of clairvoyance which enabled them to see into the spiritual world. In certain abnormal conditions of soul, the secrets of the spiritual world streamed into them and they were able to gaze into the realms of the Hierarchies. Vision of the Hierarchy of the Angels persisted the longest and was the most frequent. The angels were known as Beings belonging to the rank immediately above man."[1] Above the angels are the archangels. They are the guides of peoples and nations.

Angels and archangels are connected to all races of people. Was King Chephren able to connect with his angel, or even the archangelic world, as symbolically represented by the Horus Falcon, because he was requesting help in the guidance and protection of his people?

Today the spiritual world has largely been forgotten, and as a consequence many are in the dark about the protection that is possible for children as well as adults through the world of angels. It was quite different only three hundred years ago. A study of seventeenth-century art shows that artists painted many angels. In the two examples by Murillo of *The Angels' Kitchen* (illustrations 19 and 20), the angels are shown helping the human being perform earthly duties. The support is, of course, primarily a spiritual one and not a physical earthly one, as shown in the painting, although the artist might have implied the existence of angelic help in all areas of life. When a child is connected to spiritual truths through the fairy tale and then goes to sleep, the contact with his angel is strengthened. Some people feel intuitively that it is important in a time like ours that the strongest possible contact is made between a child and his Angel. After all, it is his angel who guides and protects him throughout life. This is the reason they are called guardian angels.[2]

It is very important to know that highly evolved spirit beings like angels have no access to intellectual thought processes or thoughts devoid of spiritual content. By that is meant ordinary thoughts that arise from day-to-day thinking.[3] Such thoughts could be described as dead thoughts, or thoughts that lack creative imagination and higher inspiration.

19

20

The Miracle of San Diego, called *The Angels' Kitchen* (1646)
Bartolomé Esteban Murillo

Angel
Duccio di Buoninsegna
(1255/60–1318/19)

This reveals that the importance of fairy tales goes far beyond reading a story to children. Through the images evoked by a true fairy tale, angel beings are invited to enter our world. In turn, their participation helps to sustain the health and well-being not only of the child, but also of people around him. In his studies of fairy tales, author Rudolf Meyer said, "If we make no attempt to gain conscious knowledge of the spiritual sources from which the fairy tale pictures arose, any sense for the higher reality which their characters express will soon be extinguished."[4]

I would like to share another experience which helped to strengthen my belief in the presence of angels, angels who have been portrayed by artists as having feelings, albeit more refined than those of human beings. Duccio di Buoninsegna, a thirteenth-century Italian painter, shows this quite clearly in illustration 21.

When our youngest daughter was seven years old, a friend invited me to a theatre performance. It was meant to be a Christmas fairy tale, performed in a church in Hamburg, Germany. Nadja had been regularly attending the children's church service on Sundays and she had grown up with many stories. We did not have television, nor did we go to the movies with our children.

While we were sitting in the church observing the play, I realized that there was nothing in the performance that truly related to the fairy tale. There was a magician, who swung his wand around and supposedly conjured up different parts of well-known fairy tales, as well as the Christmas Story of Mary and Joseph and the birth of the Child Jesus. The actors ran around the altar between each new scene. There was no atmosphere created, only restlessness. Any reverence that might have lived in the children was suppressed. At best, it was a guessing game for the audience as to which story was being presented.

I was upset that the children were exposed to such irreverence, terrible acting, and distorted imagery. For two hours I struggled with the question of how I could ever explain this behavior to my child. What could I say to her? Unable to find an answer, I pleaded for help from her angel. There was still no consolation, no idea that came to me as the fragmented play ended. We left the pews and walked out into the aisle amongst many other people. The place was packed. Suddenly Nadja said in a loud voice, "Mummy, don't you think God is going to be angry with these people?"

Everyone could hear her and I had learnt a big lesson. Was every child in that church able to see through the farce? Perhaps. Perhaps not, because an angel being needs to be acknowledged in order to respond.

The fairy tale that follows is called *The Little Golden Box*. It came as an inspiration to John of Damascus in the eighth century AD and was found and retold by Herbert Hahn, a well-known German educator. This story touches on reincarnation, sleep, and death. It presents a strong moral lesson and shows how the life we lead carries its consequences in a future life.

The Little Golden Box

In a large Golden House there lived a Father with many children. One day he spoke to one of his sons, saying, "It is time for you to go out into the world." He then led his son to a long staircase with an uncountable number of steps leading downwards.

After accompanying him for a few steps he said, "Here I have to leave you. There is only one thing that I can give to you. It is a little golden box, which you may not open and must protect very carefully." He then gave a little golden box to him, and the son carefully hid it in the folds of his cloak. "Always carry it with you," said the Father. "It will guide and protect you. When you return, you will bring it back with you."

Then the Father said farewell and the son continued his descent down the long staircase. He wanted to turn back, but how astonished he was, where in place of the steps that he had just descended, he saw an impenetrable steep black wall, while before him appeared a dark sea.

He did not know whether to go on, when suddenly he saw far in the distance a small boat coming towards him. It had no oars, no potential for steering, and no mast. It came up to him and without words seemed to invite him to get in. He could do nothing else. Seeing that his way back was barred by the steep wall, he stepped into the little boat, which carried him out to sea so quickly that soon the black wall disappeared from sight.

At first, the journey was very calm, but then a fresh breeze arose. It intensified until finally it became a violent storm. The little boat was hurled from one side to the other like a nutshell. The son could neither hear nor see; he could only hang on to the sides of the boat. Suddenly there was an enormous jerk. The boat had been thrown against a rock, resulting in a hole that was letting the water gush in. Quickly, it began to sink.

The son knew that he would drown if he stayed in the boat. But where was safety? If anywhere, it must be in the open sea! He pressed his golden box against his heart and jumped without fear into the waves. As soon as the waves received him, something wonderful happened. The storm and the terrible tossing and whirling stopped, and all the waves began to move in the same direction. The little golden box carried him as if he were held by big strong arms. It is difficult to say for how long he swam, but finally a wave carried him onto the beach of an island.

When he sat up and looked around, he saw many people coming to greet him. They called out, "Our new king has arrived!" Before he was able to think what was happening, they placed a crown on his head and a beautifully embroidered cape around his shoulders. Amidst shouts and cheers he was carried aloft to the castle. Then, as if by magic, drummers, flautists, and trumpeters accompanied him straight into a banquet hall, followed by a huge crowd. It was a feast indeed, the likes of which he had never experienced before. The whole place was lit by candles and the food was plentiful. Musicians played their instruments while actors performed. Everyone talked, toasted, and laughed, and yet no one was paying any attention to the stranger who had just arrived and sat there terrified! The music and noise became unbearably loud. He had no idea what to make of it all.

As he looked around the table, he saw an old man with a long white beard and perceptive eyes. He was looking in a kindly, yet sad manner at the young king. The son stood up and without anyone noticing went to him indicating that he would like to speak to him alone. They departed into a quiet room and there he asked the old man, "Can you tell me the meaning of all of this?"

"I can, My King. Every year a young man finds his way to the island, and for one year he is served, spoiled, and pampered. When the year is over, exactly to the hour, all the fun ends and all the feasting is finished. Then, the same people who welcomed him and who cared for him tear away his crown, rip off his cloak, and knock him off the throne! In the same state as he had arrived, he now has to go back to the beach. The boat comes but he cannot stand or sit in it; he can only lie. It takes him away to a desert island where everything is grey, silent, and lifeless. There is no little worm in the earth, nor a mosquito in the air. Never has a bird sung a song in this place! Yes, it is the end," said the old man and lowered his eyes.

"This is terrible," exclaimed the young king. "Why would all this feasting and celebrating end in such a way? Is there anything I can do?"

"I have told you all that I may say; everything else you need to find out for yourself. But it is a good sign that you have asked right away on the first day! Up to now none of the new kings has done that!" While he spoke this, his eyes lit up.

The young king thanked the old man for his advice and immediately went into the festive rooms to stop the music and send all the servants, the cooks and celebrating crowd home. "If I am their king, they might as well see what I think," he thought. Then, he withdrew into his bedchamber and began to think about all that had happened to him. He realized that fear would not help him. Instead he decided to meet courageously whatever might arise in the future. He knelt down to pray, and before he fell asleep, he laid the golden chest under his pillow.

During the night he had a strange dream and heard a familiar voice saying to him, "Go and visit the poor, the sick, and those who are lonely." It touched his heart, and when he awoke in the morning, he knew what he had to do. He declined the coach drawn by six white horses that was going to take him on a joyride and instead took a very simple carriage. He chose a doctor and a servant as helpers to take with him.

From that time onward, he followed the advice given in his dream. He went into the huts where the poor lived and into the prisons where the prisoners were chained to rocks. They were left all alone and there was very little food for them. As time passed, he realized that suffering and misery on his island was infinitely great for some of his people. He had enough work to do for weeks, even months. Day and night he was conscious of his dream, and the words he had heard did not let him rest or sleep.

The courtiers in the castle were unhappy and said, "We do not know whether we have a king or not." Yet the faces of the common people in the streets were smiling. For many it was as if they saw the sun for the first time. Time passed quickly and, after half a year had gone by, the king once again met the old counsellor who looked at him in an encouraging way. This gave him strength because he believed he was going in the right direction. But then when he met him again later, he saw concern in the old man's face and decided to ask for his advice.

"Have I done the right thing?" he asked.

"I believe that you did," replied the old man. "But perhaps not everything has been done that could have been accomplished." At this the old man stopped speaking and the king realized that he would not hear any more from him. Either he did not want to, or it was not allowed that the old man say anything else.

Late into the night the king thought about what he could have overlooked. What had he not done? Then he remembered that for quite some time he had not placed his little golden box under his pillow. This night he did, and after praying for a very long time, he fell asleep.

During the night he heard the familiar voice which spoke to him, "Have ships built! Fill them with everything that can sprout, bloom, and give fruit. Put them out to sea, to wherever the wind carries them. No one should be on board!"

When he awoke, the sun was rising. Carefully he gathered all the words that he had heard and kept them safely in his heart. On the same day he called the workmen and the shipbuilding commenced. When the ships were ready to sail, he filled them with plants, fruit and trees, grains, and seeds. People could not believe what was happening as ship after ship sailed out onto the ocean without captains. In the meantime, the king continued to look after all the poor and the sick.

Finally, the year was over and the king thought about every word that he had heard from the wise old man. He was prepared to face whatever was coming. He knelt and prayed just as he had done every morning and carried the golden box close to his heart. Suddenly it became very quiet. "Now they will come to take everything away from me," thought the king.

When the door opened, there was just one man, whom he recognized as a former starving prisoner. He knew him well. Kindly, he spoke to the king, "The hour has come, My King, and the highest law of this island is powerful indeed. We must now say goodbye. There is not one hand that will take your crown away from you or remove your gown. You are free to do it by yourself and then I will accompany you on your path to the boat."

Without hesitation the king did what was required of him. He was led through the streets where many people lined both sides. They thanked him in deep silence with loving hearts and outstretched hands for all that he had done for them. When he reached the beach, he saw the boat. The sea was calm; there was not a wave, nor breeze in the air. The boat approached as if invisible hands moved it. When it had arrived, the son thought once more about the great law of the island. Then he climbed into the boat, lay down, and immediately entered into a beautiful dream.

When he woke up, he did not know for how long he had been sailing. It felt as though the boat had bumped onto a sandy beach, and he thought that he had reached the grey desolate island. Slowly he sat up, got out of the boat, and took a few steps. How astonished he was! There was no barrenness and it was not grey either. Everywhere there were green meadows, trees were in blossom, birds sang, butterflies circled around colorful flowers, and seedlings were thriving in the fields. The son wiped his eyes and thought, "This could not be the grey, barren island of which the old man spoke." It did not come to him immediately that this was the result of the large ships that he, as king, had sent out to sea, and that invisible hands had planted and cared for all the plants and seedlings. In this way, the entire island had been transformed.

Then, when he turned to look out upon the sea, he saw once again the large steep, black wall. As if by powerful invisible hands, the wall was removed and he saw the many steps going up and up. From above he heard the voice of his Father, which he now recognized, and with indescribable joy he immediately began to climb.

On reaching the top, his Father stretched his arms out to him, asking, "Did you bring the golden box with you?"

"Yes, Father, and I have not opened it as you asked," he replied.

"Well done, my son. Now you may open it."

Looking inside the little box, the son was filled with joy at seeing an image of his Father's Mansion with all its golden halls, and all of his brothers and sisters as they walked in and out and sat all around a large round table. All of this he had carried with him without realizing its treasure!

He was still in a blessed, joyful state when he heard his Father say to him, "Now, also look at the underside of the lid." Here was a new wonder for the son, for he saw all the colors and characteristics of the island where he had been as king, and he also saw the friends that he had made and the people he had met. They all appeared real, and the old man, his counsellor, smiled at him. His eyes spoke, so that the son could feel it in his heart.

The Father, too, smiled. "You see," he said to his son, "from now on you will carry all of them in your little golden box, just as you have carried your Father's Mansion. The more you think about gratitude and love, the closer they will be to you. You have completed your journey successfully. Now come into your Father's Mansion. It is good that you rest for a while before I send you on yet another journey." The son was glad to be home once again and did as the Father suggested.

The Fourfold Human Being

The ideas that follow are taken from anthroposophy and can also be found in numerous works of art throughout the ages. They may be worth considering as possible explanations to questions concerning the meaning of the fairy tale of *The Little Golden Box*.

Every human being receives guidance from his guardian angel, and lives not only one life, but repeatedly returns to earth; in other words, every human being reincarnates. This spiritual knowledge, carried forward from the ancient past, is supported by different world religions. Rudolf Steiner said the following about reincarnation: "What is of particular importance for modern man is the gaining of conviction with regard to reincarnation and karma. The way in which men gain this conviction, how they succeed in spreading the thought of reincarnation and karma—it is this, which from now onwards will essentially transform modern life, will create new modes of life, an entirely new social life, of the kind that is necessary if human culture is not to decline but rise to a higher level."[5]

A more detailed explanation can be found in Rudolf Steiner's *Theosophy*.[6] In this book he explains that a human being in his simplest form is in fact a fourfold being. He has a physical body that can be seen, weighed, and measured and is comparable to the mineral world. In addition, he has in common with the world of plants, what is called a life body or etheric body. It is called a body because it contains formative forces and is closely aligned to the physical body. In addition, man has an astral body with which the soul is united, and an ego—the individual self.

The flowing and streaming etheric life forces are beautifully depicted in Greek art. One of the most powerful examples is the sculpture from the Parthenon, *Hestia, Dione, and Aphrodite* (illustration 22). Rudolf Steiner pointed out that the Greeks could feel their life forces streaming through their hands when they looked at the statue of a god in their temple.[7] There are people today

22
Hestia, Dione, and Aphrodite
ca. 470 BC
Parthenon, Greece

who are also aware of these life forces and use their gift for healing. When a person dies, the life force, together with its higher members, the astral body and the ego, leave the physical body. In *The Death of Niobide* (illustration 23), we see the etheric body in the shape of a cloth falling away from Niobide at the moment of her death. On the other hand, in *The Birth of Aphrodite* (illustration 24), angels are clothing Aphrodite's physical body with the etheric or life body.

Rudolf Steiner pointed out that a refined etheric essence, brought about by everything that a person has been able to transform during life on earth, such as weaknesses in character, habits, or poor memory, remains after death. It belongs to the human biography, remains with the individual throughout all future incarnations, and contributes to the evolution of the earth.[8]

The astral body is that which harbors all joys and sorrows, concerns, and frustrations, in short, the entire realm of feeling or soul life. Man's astral body is composed of two parts: a part that remains untransformed and connected to lower animal impulses and desires, and a purified part which is the result of spiritual work carried out during life on earth. The transformed astral body will connect to the etheric essence after death, becoming part of man's future biography.

23
The Death of Niobide
ca. 460 BC

24
The Birth of Aphrodite
Ludovisi throne
ca. 470 BC, Greek

Observe what lives in the sculpture by Ivan Martos, *Tombstone of Princess Sophia Volkonskaya*, (illustration 25). Notice that the cloth beneath the vase is knotted. The vase may be perceived as a picture for the little golden box, and the knot of cloth beneath it is the gathered essence of the etheric and astral.

The ego, which expresses individuality, together with the feeling life or astral body, and the etheric and physical bodies, form the complete human being.

A child who listens to fairy tales is presented with the opportunity to nourish his world of feeling. This in turn will assist him in his educational pursuits and will help him to develop in a balanced way as a member of society.

25
Tombstone of
Princess Sophia Volkonskaya
1792–1862
Ivan Martos

Reincarnation and Karma in a Fairy Tale

Anthroposophy can indeed help to lift the veil that envelopes the story of *The Little Golden Box*. This fairy tale describes the soul's journey through the gates of birth and death. The golden box is an image of what one carries on the journey into and out of incarnations—an etheric, spiritual substance which consists of everything that has developed over several lifetimes. Learning to be compassionate and to be clear in thinking or improving one's memory are just a few of such life achievements. After each incarnation a page is added to the Book of Life. This is what creates the karmic disposition for a life either rich or poor in talents and qualities. In other words, what a person does on earth makes a difference not only for that person's own future, but also for the future of others.

All the initiatives undertaken by the young king in the story appear as plants or nourishing grains. All striving that lives in a human being can also be pictured as seedlings that are sent out to sea so that they might transform an island. The seeds may not always grow into full plants in one lifetime, but the plants' continued development may be taken up in a future incarnation.

In this fairy tale, one is shown that the hero had a rich life, for he strived to do whatever was necessary in any given situation. He also experienced a spiritual life pondering life's questions in relation to a higher world and he felt compassion for the suffering of others. That, in turn, connected him to the voice that he heard—the Father's voice.[9] Therefore, when the king departs from the island, the boat is comfortable, the sea is calm, and everyone is grateful to him.

The fairy tale of *The Little Golden Box* describes the qualities that a person must develop to fulfill his or her life. The metaphors that are given can be recognized easily. There is, for example, the Golden House with the loving Father and many children. One of the sons descends the uncountable steps to his birth on earth. A black wall separates him from the spiritual world, symbolic of the barrier that exists between the two worlds. As we are born onto the earth's plane, we lose our memory of the spiritual world. In Greek mythology, water is used as a metaphor for this separation. For example, the river Lethe that flows through Hades causes the loss of memory of the past. Hades is the world of the departed spirits, and it is through the river Lethe that the living are separated from the dead.

In the beginning of the fairy tale, the son's descent down the many stairs is calm but when he climbs into the little boat, a storm arises. The boat is damaged, springs a leak, and threatens to sink. It is pointed out in the story that it is important to be fearless. When the son jumps into the waves, the storm calms down immediately. His courage is rewarded as indicated by the waves guiding him to shore. That is what the fairy tale tells us. The creator of the fairy tale must have felt that the human being will be protected even in the most dangerous of situations if there is trust, devotion, and courage.

When the son finally arrives on the beach, one may also say on the earth, he is embraced with love and care as a king on earth and carried to the banquet that is given in his honor. There, everything that the earth can offer is available, including food, art, and music. The mood is one of rejoicing. He has no idea what to make of it all and struggles with the questions that arise. The physical enjoyment of song, dance, and earthly food combined with the great noise may convince the reader, as it did the young king, that in this environment there is a lack of interest in the spirit and in any kind of striving that could make the earth a better place for everyone.

The reader's attention is drawn to two important character traits possessed by the young king: obedience through heartfelt faith and an inquisitive mind—the king asks many questions. In turn he trusts and obeys the voice which tells him of the misery amongst the people in his land. He has the courage to act instantly. When he asks questions of the wise old man, who can be seen as an initiate,[10] he shows humility and a sincere wish to understand. Twice he receives advice and encouragement, but without any details as to what to do, where to go, or how to do it. He thinks deeply, he prays, and then he listens to the voice that comes to him. When the voice of inspiration comes, he takes it into his heart.

This could occur to every person in everyday life, if he or she is led by conscience to work in the world for the good of others. There are many people who volunteer their time and efforts towards fighting human injustice, or for the protection of animals, or for the preservation of the environment. In their own neighborhoods they help the blind, or the elderly, or organize food programs for the less fortunate. When they have done all they can to ease the suffering of others, when they have followed their path without shying away from responsibility, then there will be, just like in the story, many outstretched hands acknowledging in gratitude everything that they have accomplished. Plants and seeds placed on ships need no captains, because they find their own way to the island. Similarly, good deeds carried out by man on earth reach the spiritual world unaided. They will blossom and be cared for by guardian angels.

At the end of the story the attention is drawn once more to the important little golden box that represents the etheric and astral essence, for it contains all the memories of past lives, all the feelings and will impulses that will now be woven into a new karma. This indeed allows one to reflect on cosmic laws.[11] There are consequences for misdeeds, but there is always free will and loving forgiveness. One imagines in this fairy tale how caringly and lovingly the Father welcomes back the son, before sending him out again. Likewise, in the future, men will lovingly take the concerns and needs of others into their hearts. At that time, compassion and commitment will play a far greater role in society. The following words are from Rudolf Steiner:

> A time will come—and it must not pass unnoticed—when out of the spiritual world men will receive an impulse through their Angel that will kindle a far deeper interest in every individual human being than we are inclined to have today. This enhanced interest in our fellow men will not unfold in the subjective, leisurely way that people would prefer, but by a sudden impetus a certain secret will be inspired into man from the spiritual side, namely, what the other man really is. …That is what will particularly affect the social life.[12]

The fairy tale of *The Little Golden Box* points to this future. Just as the young king was able to make a difference in his kingdom, perhaps on earth too, compassion will predominate. Meanwhile, we live in a time when every human being has to leave the earthly kingdom after having encountered many life situations that need karmic balancing because, as the story points out, the highest law is powerful, indeed! This is movingly expressed in William Blake's drawing, *The Lord God Writing the Law* (illustration 26). In this work, Blake depicts souls that are falling while others rise upward.

Our time calls for an increased awareness and understanding of our connection to the cosmos. Whereas the study of the external physical world becomes ever drier, intellectual and abstract, the study of spiritual life will become more heartfelt and take on a deeper significance. It will develop into the quality of prayer, not in a one-sided sentimental sense but by virtue of its own nature. Man will come to know that what he has experienced between his last death and a new birth now lives within him and will be felt as the inner riches of his life.

26
*The Lord God
Writing the Law*
William Blake
(1757–1827)

The Cross of Francis of Assisi, 13th c.

3 The Firebird

Our birth is but a sleep and a forgetting;
Our soul that rises with us, our life's Star,
Hath had elsewhere its setting,
And cometh from afar:
Not in entire forgetfulness,
And not in utter nakedness,
But trailing clouds of glory do we come
From God, who is our home:
Heaven lies about us in our infancy!

– William Wordsworth

In this excerpt from his poem, "Ode: Intimations of Immortality,"[1] Wordsworth points out the journey of a soul's incarnation, which was the theme of the fairy tale, *The Little Golden Box*. With each incarnation, new human faculties need to be developed. In the Russian fairy tale, *The Firebird*,[2] one such faculty, the development of the will, is presented.

The Firebird

Once upon a time there lived a king and a queen. The queen gave birth to a baby boy and they named him Ivan.

Prince Ivan was special and unlike any other boy. His arms were made of gold from his hands all the way up to his elbows, and his legs were made of silver from his feet all the way up to his knees. During the day, when the sun shone, his forehead glowed golden, while at night, when the moon was out, it shone silver.

An old nurse looked after the little prince. One day she was trying to rock him to sleep and he would not close his eyes, so she called out to the queen: "Please come, Your Majesty, and rock your little prince to sleep."

The queen sat by the cradle, but she was unable to help him fall asleep and so she called to the king: "Come, Your Majesty, come and rock your baby to sleep."

The king was happy to sing a lullaby to the little prince. He sang about a beautiful princess who would one day be his bride, and he described her in riddles to which there were no obvious answers:

> Sleep, little son, and slumber long.
> Grow through boyhood tall and strong.
> Into the great world you shall ride
> And win a princess for your bride—
> The lovely Princess Vasilissa,
> Daughter of three mothers,
> Darling of three grandmothers,
> Sister of nine brothers.
> Her beauty dazzles like the sun
> Rising from the sea.
> You shall strive till she is won,
> And she your wife shall be.

It did not take the little prince long to fall asleep, and he slept deeply for nine whole years, nine months, nine weeks, and nine days. When he finally awoke, he went to the king and told him that he wanted to ride out into the world.

"I want to go to the four corners of the earth," he said, "to find my bride, the beautiful Princess Vasilissa, daughter of three mothers, darling of three grandmothers, and sister of nine brothers, a princess who is so beautiful that she can be compared to the radiance of the sun when he rises from the sea."

The king answered him, saying, "My son, you are too young, you have not yet had a chance to learn from life and become wise. The world is dangerous and you might die or lose your way."

Then Prince Ivan responded, "I am old enough and I know enough. Please give me your blessing. I want to go out into the world to find the beautiful Princess Vasilissa. If you refuse to give me your blessing, I will go without it."

"Just a moment," said the king. "I need to measure and weigh you in order to find out if you are really strong enough." When he had measured the prince and found him just right in weight, in height and in width, the king and the queen felt that they had to let him go out into the world.

Prince Ivan swung himself onto a horse with a beautifully handcrafted leather saddle, took the silver bridle in his hands, and placed his feet firmly into the stirrups. He followed a road that led him through woods, across meadows, over fields, and into little villages and towns until he came to a dark forest.

Beside the road, at the edge of the forest, he saw a fiercely burning bush. When he looked more closely, he saw a large anthill under the bush and ants scurrying back and forth. They were trying to get their eggs to safety and were disoriented by the fire. The heat frightened them and when they saw the prince, they cried out, "Prince Ivan, please help us or we shall all burn to death, our eggs and babies too!"

The prince jumped off his horse, cut the bush at its roots and put out the fire.

"Thank you, thank you," said the eldest ant as she came up to him. "In return, we would like to give you some advice."

"That would be most welcome," said the prince, and he smiled at the little creatures.

The ant continued, "Prince Ivan, remember never to turn back until you have come to the end of your journey."

"What a strange piece of advice to give to someone like me," he replied. "I have set out to find the beautiful Princess Vasilissa, and I certainly will not turn back until I have found her. Thank you kindly." He courteously acknowledged the ant and rode on.

For a long time he rode across meadows, over dales, and through dense forests until he came upon the deep blue ocean. On the sandy beach he saw a fish flopping about in distress. It had obviously been tossed up by the waves and could not make its way back into the water.

"Help me, Prince Ivan, help me!" the fish begged. "I must get back into the water; otherwise I will die."

The prince leapt off his horse, grasped the tail of the fish, and threw it back into the sea. The fish did not swim away. Instead he thanked Prince Ivan and then offered him some advice. "Listen carefully, Prince Ivan. Never let go of what you have caught."

The fish's head disappeared beneath the waves and the prince was left thinking, "That is truly strange advice. I will not let go of what I have caught. After all, I am going to have the Princess Vasilissa as my bride!"

Then Prince Ivan climbed back onto his horse and continued on his journey. He crossed the sea and came to a high mountain where he saw a large oak tree. Stopping there, he jumped off his horse and settled down to have a rest.

When he awoke he noticed two young ravens that had fallen from their nest. They were squawking raucously. "Please, please, help us, Prince Ivan, or we shall die. Our parents have flown away and left us to fend for ourselves. But we cannot fly yet, and as we cannot find food for ourselves, we will surely die of hunger," they cried.

Prince Ivan covered himself with some branches, and then with his bow, aimed at a deer that happened to run by. He killed it with one arrow. Now the ravens had enough to eat.

"Thank you Prince Ivan. In return, we would like to give you some advice," they said.

"You, too, want to give me advice? You cannot even fly yet!" he said. "However, good advice is always welcome."

"Take it seriously, Prince Ivan," the young ravens said. "Never refuse the request of a friend."

"This is not so very clever," said the prince. "If I helped the ants, the fish, and now you—and none of you were my friends—how could I refuse the request of someone who is already my friend?"

No one really knows for how long the prince was on the road, riding through the wide world, asking everywhere where he could find Princess Vasilissa. One day he came to a city that was draped all in black. He arrived at an inn and knocked at the door. The innkeeper opened it.

"Why is your whole city draped in black? What has happened?" Prince Ivan asked.

The innkeeper knew that the young man before him must have come from afar. "Oh," he said, "you have not heard? The king's daughter, the beautiful Princess Vasilissa, has disappeared. She is lost like a needle in a haystack. The whole city is in mourning because no one can find her."

Prince Ivan was so happy to have finally made contact with people who knew her that he did not even say "Goodbye" or "Thank you," but hurriedly swung himself into the saddle and rode his horse straight to the castle.

The king was surprised to see such a handsome youth with arms of gold up to his elbows, legs of silver up to his knees, and golden sunlight glowing from his forehead. He was astonished when the prince told him that he had come from far away to find the lovely Princess Vasilissa, the king's own beloved daughter, because he wanted to take her home with him as his bride.

"You may have my daughter as your bride," the king said. "But first you must find her. Many have looked for her, but no one yet has been able to find out where she is."

"Oh, Mighty King, I shall find her," Prince Ivan replied, "even if I have to go to the four corners of the earth!"

The king was impressed and the prince set out on his horse, riding over hill and over dale, through deep forests and across wide plains. He waded across rivers and over dry prairies, and he asked everyone he thought might be able to help him where he could find the beautiful Princess Vasilissa.

No one knew, and they all shook their heads in sorrow. His hope of finding her gradually began to fade and he asked himself, "Why should I continue on this path, if no one can help me?"

When at last he was ready to give up and return home, he remembered the advice of the ants: *Never turn back until you have come to the end of the journey.*

"Perhaps that was good advice after all," he said to himself, and he continued along the path thinking, "I will persevere!"

Prince Ivan was tired and weary when one evening he arrived at a beautiful garden full of flowers. He tied his horse to a tree and lay down under it. He felt the protection of its branches and soon fell asleep on the soft grass. For how long he slept he did not know, but he awakened to the most beautiful sound of music. It was as if angels were singing all around him.

When he looked up, outlined against the night sky he saw that the tree was laden with large golden apples which were swaying in the wind. It was these swaying apples that were making the beautiful sound. When he was fully awake, he rose to his feet in wonder, reached up, and tried to pick one of the golden apples.

All of a sudden, he saw a bird, filled with radiant light, perched on the tree. Its feathers were a fiery golden color. The bird was eating the golden apples, and all the while a gentle breeze filled the air. "What a beautiful bird!" he exclaimed, and stood in wonder before the magnificent creature as it sang:

> How sweet are the apples,
> These golden apples,
> Sweet as the smile of Princess Vasilissa,
> Daughter of three mothers,
> Darling of three grandmothers,
> Sister of nine brothers.
> Her beauty dazzles
> Like the sun
> Rising from the sea.

Prince Ivan listened with surprise and excitement as the song continued:

> How sweet are the apples,
> These golden apples,
> Sweet as the smile of Princess Vasilissa,

Who was carried away
By the deathless magician.
Beware of Kostchei
Who lives on the blood
Of those who intrude
Where dwells the Princess
Who longs to be free.

Prince Ivan was unable to move and he felt completely overcome. Before he could come to his senses, the bird continued yet again:

How sweet are these apples,
These golden apples,
Sweet as the smile of Princess Vasilissa,
Whom Prince Ivan seeks
By day and by night
In darkness and in light
On land and at sea.
He'll find her
Wherever she may be.

"This wonderful bird can help me," the prince thought. He jumped up and seizing it, said, "Now I have got you. I will never let you go."

The creature dug his claws into Prince Ivan's silver legs and beat his wings against his golden arms trying to free himself. But Prince Ivan held him firmly in his hands. When the bird realized that the prince would not let him get away, he said, "Prince Ivan, if you let me go, I will tell you where you can find the beautiful Princess Vasilissa. If you follow my advice, you will succeed in rescuing her. I am the Firebird and I alone have power over the magician Kostchei the Deathless, who has kidnapped the Princess and holds her in his black castle. Let me go and I will help you."

The prince was just about to let the Firebird go when he remembered the advice the fish had given him: *Never let go of what you have caught.*

"Thank you, fish," he thought in his mind. "That was good advice." And he held onto the bird even more saying, "I will never let you go."

"You speak wisely, Prince Ivan," said the golden bird. "Just pluck a feather from my tail and keep it with you and then please let me go. Whenever you need my help, all you have to do is wave the feather above your head and I shall come."

"Very well," said Prince Ivan. "You may put your wise and lovely head on my broad shoulders and guide me into the future with all your knowledge and wisdom." With that he plucked one of the feathers from the tail of this wondrous bird and tossed him up into the air. The bird flew up high and then vanished, leaving a golden trail behind him.

The prince once again lay down beneath the tree and fell asleep. At early dawn the next morning, he woke to the voices of twelve beautiful maidens coming towards him. They were singing a sad song. Every one of them was beautiful, but in their midst was a thirteenth who was more beautiful than all the others. When Prince Ivan saw her, he was overcome and in awe of her beauty. He walked towards her and said, "Who are you, beautiful maiden and what are you doing here in the garden of Kostchei the Deathless?"

The beautiful girl answered sadly, "I am Princess Vasilissa, daughter of three mothers, darling of three grandmothers, and sister of nine brothers. Kostchei the Deathless brought me here against my will because he wants me to be his bride."

She began to cry, saying, "Who are you and what are you doing here? No one comes here willingly. Even the wild animals and the evil ravens flee from this place. Leave quickly, my lord! The terrible magician catches whoever sets foot into this garden. He sucks the blood of his prey down to the last drop and that is the reason why he lives on forever."

"You, beautiful Princess, my lovely Vasilissa," cried Prince Ivan, "I came to free you from this fearsome magician. I am Prince Ivan, and you have been destined to be my bride since the day I was born. I have come to take you home with me. I shall not leave, and I am not afraid!"

"Whatever your destiny may be, Prince Ivan, there is no hope for me, for no one, not even you, can free me from this terrible monster. Kostchei is a powerful and strong magician. Go! Go while there is still time!"

Prince Ivan was not afraid. He sat down in the shade of the tree and drew the Princess down beside him. As they were talking together, the other girls picked the golden apples, and gradually hope began to rise in Prince Ivan. Perhaps he could find a way to overcome the magician.

The sky suddenly darkened as a huge black cloud covered the face of the sun. The girls jumped up and ran as fast as they could towards the castle. Vasilissa too had gone before the prince realized what was happening, and there standing before him was the powerful Kostchei, a repulsive man with a toothless grin that stretched from one ear to the other. He had a long nose almost reaching to his chin. He was bald except for one single hair. He wore a black cloak and carried a long stick. His eyes were full of hatred. "I know why you have come here. You wish to win the beautiful Vasilissa for your bride, but you shall not succeed. She is mine, and mine alone!" said Kostchei the magician.

The prince responded, "Yes, indeed it is true. I have come to rescue her and I shall succeed."

With a hearty laugh Kostchei said, "Many have tried before you and all of them have died. I will set you three tasks. If you can fulfill them, she will be yours. If you fail, you will forfeit your life."

"I shall fulfill the tasks," said Prince Ivan fearlessly.

"Listen carefully," said Kostchei the Deathless. "Behind my castle is a forest that is one mile wide and one mile long. By tomorrow morning I want you to fell all the trees, cut them into logs, dig up the roots, plough the earth, sow wheat, reap it, grind it, and from the flour bake pirozhki for my breakfast. If you can do this, I will give you the second task. If not, you will lose your life." Having said this, the magician was gone and only a black cloud was left in his place.

Prince Ivan had a heavy heart as he sat down under the tree. How could he ever manage such a huge task? He was close to despair. He thought he would never again feel the warmth of the sun or the gentle rain. "What can I do?" he cried in anguish.

Then he thought of the Firebird. Could this bird really help him out of his plight? He waved the feather over his head, just as the bird had told him to, and then the whole garden was filled with a murmuring sound as if swept by a gentle breeze. The magician's castle was bathed in a bright glow as though it were on fire. The Firebird alighted on the tree and asked the prince what he wanted.

"Dear Firebird, Kostchei the Deathless has given me a most difficult task. Can you help me?" asked the prince. "It is the first of three tasks. I am supposed to cut down the forest behind the castle, stack all the logs, dig out the roots, plough and sow wheat, harvest and thresh it, and bake pirozhki for his breakfast. And he wants it all done by tomorrow morning. If I do not manage it, I will lose my life."

The Firebird looked fondly at the prince and said, "I will look after everything. This is nothing to me. Just go into the castle and enjoy some time with the Princess." Before Prince Ivan could say thank you, the Firebird was gone.

When Prince Ivan came to the castle, there was darkness everywhere—all was black outside and inside. The walls were black, the furniture was black and even the light coming through the windows was dark. But when Ivan found his beloved Princess, everything seemed to be full of light. All the shadows were dispelled through being with his beautiful Princess. Perhaps this was the last evening they would ever spend together.

At the stroke of midnight Prince Ivan went to the back of the castle and could not believe his eyes. The forest was gone; instead there were piles of logs stacked up. A large field had been harvested, the stubble was still standing, and next to it there were bags of flour. Right in the middle of the cleared field there was a huge fire in which the remaining stumps were still burning.

The Firebird was watching and when he saw Prince Ivan, he said joyfully, "There, Prince Ivan, everything is ready. As for the pirozhki, Princess Vasilissa will bake them for you." With these words the Firebird leapt into the fire. In an instant all that remained of him was a pile of ashes.

Prince Ivan was shocked when he saw such a beautiful bird die. Then fear arose in him. How would he manage the other two tasks without the help of the Firebird? He did not have to worry for long because the Firebird arose from the ashes and was even more beautiful than before.

"You seem surprised, Prince Ivan," he said. "You see, this is the reason why I am called the Firebird. I bathe in fire just as you bathe in water. When you come out of your bath, you are clean and handsome, and when I arise from my bath of fire, my feathers are glossier and I am more beautiful than ever before."

Prince Ivan was happy as he carried the sacks of flour to the castle, where the Princess began making nice hot pirozhki.

When Kostchei came in the morning, he was astonished to find pirozhki on the table, and when he looked out of the window to find the task fulfilled, he was furious. "You will not manage to fulfill the next task. It is so much harder," he screamed. "By tomorrow morning you must dig a lake behind the castle, seventeen miles long and seventeen miles wide. It must be so deep that not only boats, but also great galleys will be able to sail on it. You must fill that lake with water, build across it a bridge with a gilded rail, and on that bridge plant an apple tree every three yards. One must be in bloom and the next must bear apples. They may not be ordinary apples but they must be golden ones with pearls inside instead of seeds. These are the kind that the Firebird eats. Underneath each tree there must be a spring of fresh water, so that when I go for a stroll, I shall be able to sit and rest in the shade and have a drink. If you manage to complete this task, I will give you your third task. If you do not, you know what your fate will be." With these words Kostchei the Deathless departed.

This time Prince Ivan did not wait but waved the feather over his head as he had before. At once he heard the murmuring sound like the passing breath of a breeze. The light around him became bright as if the castle were on fire, and suddenly the Firebird appeared. "What is it you want, Prince Ivan?" the golden-winged bird asked. "Were you given a new task?"

"Yes, indeed," replied the prince. "I am supposed to dig a lake behind the castle seventeen miles long and seventeen miles wide and fill it with water. It must be so deep that not only small boats can sail on it, but also big galleys. Across the water I am to build a bridge with a gilded rail, and on that bridge I am to plant an apple tree every three yards so that when one blooms, the next bears apples. These may not be ordinary apples, but golden ones of the kind that you like to eat. Underneath each tree there is to be a spring of fresh water, so that when Kostchei goes for a walk, he will be able to sit and rest in the shade. He likes to drink the cool spring water when he is hot and thirsty."

"Oh, this is nothing to me," said the Firebird. "In the morning you will see that everything is ready. Now go and comfort the beautiful Princess Vasilissa. She is weeping because of you."

Quickly Prince Ivan thanked the Firebird and went to find the Princess Vasilissa whom he found by the window sitting sad and forlorn. As soon as she saw him, she smiled.

In the early morning light, when the prince looked out of the castle window, the nature of the landscape had changed. There, glittering in the rays of the morning sun, was a huge lake with galleys and boats sailing on it. Across the middle there was a bridge with an apple tree every three yards, one in bloom and the next with golden apples. Underneath them was a row of freshwater springs. Prince Ivan was overjoyed and made his way to the garden.

Soon Kostchei appeared and at the sight that met his eyes he exclaimed in anger, "So you have fulfilled the second task also! But you have not won your Princess yet, because the third task is the most difficult. Listen well! By tomorrow you must bring Death to me!"

Prince Ivan responded, "Why wait until tomorrow! Why not now?" He drew his sword, and struck the magician fiercely on his head. The sword bounced off as if his head were made of steel, and Kostchei just laughed at him.

"Hey! Not so easy, is it?" The prince did not know what to do. "Have you forgotten that I am Kostchei the Deathless? Prince Ivan, you cannot bring death to me and now you will lose your life!"

Then the magician waved his hand—fire, smoke, and the most horrible monsters, giants, headless ogres, ugly witches, lizards, devils and dragons, instantly surrounded the prince. They attacked Prince Ivan with piercing claws, cackling and shrieking. Prince Ivan fought bravely with all his skill, using his sword but to no avail. When he cut the lizard in half, immediately there were two in its place. He cut the dragon's head off with one stroke, but in its place were two heads. He pierced the giant through, but another giant leapt out of the gaping wound. There seemed no way out of this terrible fight.

Finally he remembered the Firebird. He reached for the golden feather and waved it over his head. At once the bird appeared before him and in his claw he carried a golden sword. "Take heed, Kostchei the Deathless, your death is near!" At the sound of these words, all the horrible monsters disappeared into the ground. The magician turned pale and began to shake with fear.

"Quickly now, Prince Ivan, here is the sword. You must cut me in half. Inside of me you will find a large black egg, and if you break it, you will cause the death of Kostchei."

"I cannot do that," cried Ivan. "How could I kill you? You have helped me so much."

The golden bird answered, "You must do it. Otherwise you will die. I have carried this black egg in me for a long, long time and I cannot lay it. That is why the magician kept feeding me with golden apples to keep me alive, preserving the egg of death where it could not harm him. Do it quickly!"

At this moment the prince heard the young ravens giving their advice: *Never refuse the request of a friend.* He cut the Firebird in half and the egg inside as well. There was a deafening roar, and Kostchei the Deathless fell to the ground—dead.

The Firebird's slain body burned with a bright flame until only ashes were left. Then once again he arose and, soaring into the air, he looked more beautiful than ever. After circling twice over Prince Ivan's head, he rose as a golden cloud in the sky and then was gone, to be seen no more.

All darkness vanished, the walls turned red, the furniture blue, and the dishes silver. All the rooms were filled with light and before Prince Ivan stood a hundred knights whom Kostchei had killed and who now came to life again. Following the knights came the twelve beautiful girls who had been held prisoner in the castle by the magician. Then coming towards him was the most beautiful of all, Princess Vasilissa, daughter of three mothers, darling of three grandmothers, sister of nine brothers, her beauty dazzling like the sun rising from the sea. Everyone in turn came up to thank Prince Ivan for having freed them.

The knights then brought a horse and Prince Ivan lifted his lovely bride up onto its back. Then he laid his beautiful leather saddle on his own handsome horse. He looped the silver bridle over its head, pulled the silken girths tight, adjusted the stirrups, swung himself into the saddle, and away they rode.

They travelled for many, many miles, high and low, over mountains and valleys, fields and meadows, through forests and clearings, across streams and rivers until they finally came to the city ruled by Princess Vasilissa's father, the king. When the king saw her, he was so happy that he wept tears of joy and so did her three mothers and three grandmothers and nine brothers. The black drapes were taken down by the people and replaced with cloths of red. Then there was great feasting and rejoicing, the like of which no one has seen, or ever will.

After the old king died, the land was governed wisely and well by King Ivan and Queen Vasilissa. If they have not died, they are still living today.

The world of the fairy tale is full of wonder. Its pictures find a direct path to the soul of the reader where they can be taken up into consciousness and pondered. Individual imaginations, such as the prince with his golden arms and a bird that bathes in fire, can in the mind of an adult reader awaken questions that beg to be answered. Why gold? What is the meaning of fire? Both of these elements are also found in other fairy tales. Without deeper insight or answers about the meaning of fairy tales, more and more people will find their content appropriate only for children. They do not realize that children intuitively feel the adult's lack of interest and that this diminishes the healing value of the fairy tale.

When an attempt is made to allow the fairy tales to live through spiritual science, and not only through intellectual interpretation, then beings of the higher world from which the fairy tales originate connect with both the storyteller and the listeners.

A Human Ego Expresses Itself through Thinking, Feeling, and Willing

To begin with, it is important to take a closer look at the faculties with which a human being meets the world. A human being expresses himself through his thoughts and feelings and, of course, through his will. Rudolf Steiner said, "Thus we see that, in the true sense of the word, we are really awake only in our sense-perceptions and our life of ideas; in the life of feeling we are so near to sleeping as to be dreaming; and in the life of will we are always fast asleep."[3]

Taking a closer look at these three faculties, one may readily agree that a person today is fully conscious only in his life of ideas—his thinking. Regarding his feeling life, he may discover emotions with underlying intentions, feelings yet unknown to him. They can be described as dreamlike. For example, a person may see an elderly woman, a neighbor, walking down the street carrying heavy bags. He offers to help carry them because he thinks that he feels sorry for her. In reality, however, what lies hidden in the soul could be the wish to be recognized as a Good Samaritan. Another example is a wife who has been physically abused by her husband and says to him, "I am sorry. I love you. Please don't leave me." Is this really love or an unseen fear of being abandoned? These motives are not fully conscious; they live within the human being, but in a dreaming way.

If one reviews the third faculty, that of the will, one might say, "I will go into the garden and do some digging." This thought represents a conscious decision: However, the activity of digging is an action of the will, of which one is not fully conscious. One digs automatically without being conscious of every movement of one's limbs. When a two-year-old stomps his foot, it is an act of will, also without consciousness.

Consider the immediate reaction that occurs, for example, following a window that is suddenly blown open: A person's consciousness is directed towards the physical discomfort caused by the noise and the draught. When the person gets up to shut the window, is he or she fully conscious of every movement of the hand and foot while moving forward to close it, or is this simply an involuntary reaction? Rudolf Steiner said, "The nearer we come to the impulses of will, the further we descend into the subconscious, the dark realms into which we sink completely when consciousness is engulfed in deep, dreamless sleep-life."[4]

The fairy tale of *The Firebird* is the story of an initiation of the will. In other words, through the fairy tale one is given an imagination of a path that leads to the awakening and transformation of one's will. This path can bring consciousness to all that one is doing, to every thought, every feeling, and every action. This endeavor is a very difficult one, but the reward is the highest.

With an awakened will, it becomes possible for a person to work consciously on his or her own future. The consequence, as shown by the activities of Prince Ivan, is to contribute to the well-being of others and, in the greater context, to the whole of mankind. If Prince Ivan was successful in overcoming the challenges presented to him by the evil Kostchei, it was possible only through his constantly active will. Overcoming Kostchei is symbolic for overcoming evil in oneself. This is not easily done.

The Reality of a Higher Self

Upon entering more deeply into the story of *The Firebird*, one finds that an important question arises: Who is the beautiful and mysterious Princess Vasilissa? In order to find an answer, one might begin by asking yet another question: How is Princess Vasilissa portrayed by those who know her?

Much can be said about her, but the king, keeping the Princess veiled in mystery, is the first to describe her with the following puzzling statement: "She is the daughter of three mothers, darling of three grandmothers, and sister of nine brothers." The king's authority and wisdom lend weight to the mysterious lines that describe Princess Vasilissa's ancestry. He also predicts that Prince Ivan will one day take her for his bride.

Another interesting occurrence, later in the story, points to the significance of Princess Vasilissa. It is the innkeeper's lament, when he says that with her disappearance, beauty and light vanished from the kingdom. The innkeeper attends to people's physical well-being by providing them with food and a place of rest. Why would the innkeeper express his awareness of Princess Vasilissa's importance? His interest reveals that freeing the Princess will not only be a personal gain for Prince Ivan, but will also be of great benefit to all residents of the city and to the land which was draped in black to mourn her disappearance.

This fairy tale lives in the spirit realm, and the light which is mentioned is not a physical light, but a spiritual one. The loss of spirituality slowly results in despondency and a lack of well-being. In the early sixteenth century, Matthias Grünewald painted such an idea in the *Isenheim Altarpiece* (illustration 27, next page). In the detail of the painting, we can see the darkness in the clouds created by evil spirits, but we can also perceive the light that streams down from the spiritual world to a pure soul. It spreads into and encompasses the whole environment.

Finally, Princess Vasilissa confirms her unusual lineage when she meets the prince. She herself tells him who she is, and surprisingly uses the same words as the king: "I am Princess Vasilissa, daughter of three mothers, darling of three grandmothers, and sister of nine brothers." She is fully conscious of her elevated position and of her beauty.

Three Mothers, Three Grandmothers, and Nine Brothers

The reader hears this puzzling description three times. What is the meaning of the three mothers, the three grandmothers, and the nine brothers? No human being born on earth can have three mothers! It can be said, however, that each human being is born into a world of linear time and that the growth and development of the soul is interwoven with the past, the present, and the future. Are the three mothers, therefore, a conscious choice by the storyteller as a metaphor for the past, present, and future? Perhaps there are other answers, but this one invites an interesting idea.

27
Virgin and Child
detail from the *Isenheim Altarpiece*
(1515) Colmar, France
Matthias Grünewald

How is one to understand the image of the three grandmothers? It is important to realize that in the supersensible world genders do not exist. It has been indicated in the fairy tale of *Little Red Riding Hood* that the grandmother was chosen as a metaphor for mankind's spiritual origin, or God. However, here we have three grandmothers! The number three is a sacred number and was well-known in ancient wisdom. It expresses the beginning, the middle, and the ending of all things. To ancient man the universe appeared to be divided into three regions represented by three gods. The number three is sacred in other traditions and elsewhere, for example among the Vedic people of India. If the fairy tale is imagined in the light of Christianity, then the Trinity comes to mind as the Father, Son, and Holy Spirit.

A possible answer to the mystery concerning the nine brothers leads us to a representative of the earliest Christian tradition, Dionysius the Areopagite,[5] who

28
La Ronde des Élus
Fra Angelico
15th c.

lived in Athens in the first century AD. In his teachings about the celestial hierarchies, he spoke of nine ranks of spiritual beings who were involved in the creation of the human being. Rudolf Steiner, in his lectures "Universe, Earth, and Man,"[6] also described nine hierarchical ranks that not only assisted in man's creation but guide and protect the whole of mankind.

Angelic Beings of the First Hierarchy have been depicted in art throughout the centuries. Fra Angelico's *La Ronde des Élus* (illustration 28) shows them hand-in-hand with man. Many other artists painted even higher ranks of spiritual beings, such as the Cherubim with their four wings and Seraphim with six (illustration 29).

Up to this point in our discussion of Princess Vasilissa, she appears to be only a fairy tale character. Is there anything in the innermost composition of a human being that compares to the

29
Seraphim
Byzantine
Abbey Church
Hurez, Romania

wisdom, beauty, and light of Vasilissa? Yes, Princess Vasilissa serves as a description for what is called the Higher Self.[7]

According to Spiritual Science, achieving marriage with the Higher Self, which will occur for mankind in the distant future, is called reaching the development of Spirit Self. It is an evolutionary step which the angels have already achieved.[8] Striving for truth, beauty, and goodness, learning to forgive, acting out of love, and training one's thinking, feeling, and willing through soul exercises carry the greatest rewards that any human being can achieve. These attributes will forever be connected to a person's individual biography and will be expressed through future talents and skills. What is brought to earth from former incarnations will be further worked on in connection with higher beings. In Rudolf Steiner's words, this possibility of working on oneself was given to mankind by "a world directive full of wisdom." We live in a time when man is beginning to develop his consciousness soul. Many people have consciously taken on the task of defending forests against their destruction, protecting wildlife and the environment, promoting healthy living, and advocating more meaningful education.

The knowledge that man is part of a cosmic whole can give much inner strength to an individual struggling in today's world. According to anthroposophical knowledge, the next major developmental step for mankind is the individual's striving for the transformation of the soul life. Is the human being prepared to accept this challenge? This is the most important question that sounds forth in our present day.

Those with spiritual interests recognize divine caring and guidance in many personal situations throughout life. For example, being saved from an accident, meeting the right person at the right time, or finding the right book which opens at an answer being sought—all of these are instances of higher beings' gently leading a person on a path to the spirit.

A New Look at the Zodiac

In a fifteenth-century prayer book, *Les Très Riches Heures du Duc de Berry*, there is a beautiful representation of man in the midst of the zodiacal hierarchy. This illustration is also called *Anatomical Man* (illustration 30). The nine hierarchies of spiritual beings and the Trinity, spoken of by Dionysius the Areopagite, are shown surrounding two human figures.

This picture can be considered from at least three different viewpoints. In the first instance, a human being is seen as separate male and female figures standing back to back, in harmony with the cosmos. However, the male and female duality can also be understood from a second perspective. In *The Firebird*, for instance, Prince Ivan unites in marriage with Princess Vasilissa, his higher self, and through the wedding achieves a stage of perfection. Thirdly, the human being can be viewed as undergoing the stage of gestation within a cosmic egg, surrounded by the nine hierarchies, which bestow their creative forces for the formation of new life. All three views are valid.

30
Anatomical Man from
*Les Très Riches Heures du
Duc de Berry*
15th c.

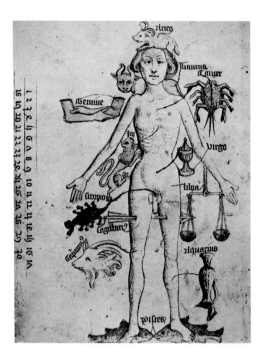

31
Zodiacal Man
from a manuscript
16th c.

Another example can be found in a sixteenth-century manuscript, *The Guild Book of the Barber Surgeons of York*, *Zodiacal Man* (illustration 31). Here profound insights into the mysteries of the zodiac are revealed. These can be further studied in anthroposophical writings.[9] These depictions show that some artists still retained knowledge of these cosmic mysteries and expressed them through their works.

At night, when we look up at the sky, we see the moon, planets and an infinite multitude of stars. However, behind the veil of sense perception, at times referred to as *maya*, there live highly evolved spiritual beings who have their abode in cosmic space occupied by zodiacal signs and planets. This mystery remains largely unknown. Most people generally know only the names of the planets and the twelve signs of the zodiac.

In illustration 31, the corresponding symbols of the zodiac have been placed on the anatomy of the human being, to which they are connected. These symbols represent the various creative spiritual forces that are united during gestation to bring about and ensure new life on earth.

The hierarchical association to the zodiac is as follows: In the Third Hierarchy, Angels are connected to Aquarius, Archangels to Capricorn, and Archai to Sagittarius. In the Second Hierarchy, the Exusiai are associated with Scorpio, Dynamis with Libra, and Kyriotetes with Virgo; and in the First Hierarchy the Thrones to Leo, Cherubim to Cancer, and Seraphim to Gemini. In relation to the hierarchies Rudolf Steiner stated, "After the archangels and angels, the arch-messengers and messengers, we shall have to place among the hierarchical ranks the Spirit of Freedom or the Spirit of Love. Counting from above downward, this is the tenth hierarchy, which, though still in a process of development, nevertheless belongs to the Divine Hierarchies."[10] In *The Firebird*, beings from the nine hierarchies are portrayed as Princess Vasilissa's nine brothers. Embedded into man's spiritual and physical constitution lies the seed that was planted by the hierarchies and that will mature during man's future evolutionary journey. This seed, as it germinates, will make man's transformation of the lower into the higher, or spirit self, possible. It is a step that, once achieved, will allow man to become conscious of hierarchical beings and their creative working, as well as to commune with them directly.

If one considers how deeply interwoven the human being is with the hierarchical world, it is understandable that the fairy tale can only provide a very limited picture.

Sun and Moon, Gold and Silver

Having unveiled a part of the mystery surrounding Princess Vasilissa, the next question might be: Who is Prince Ivan? As a representative of mankind, Prince Ivan carries in himself character traits which lie dormant in every human being. Because he has purity of soul and continues with the most sincere and persistent striving, he becomes worthy to win Princess Vasilissa. His attempt to unite with her is the essence of the story of *The Firebird*. Princess Vasilissa is a higher being than the prince. Therefore, his goal is the attainment of all that she represents.

If the prince's qualities live as seeds in every human being, then it can be assumed that whoever is interested in a path of spiritual development will be able to eventually reach the goal. In the fairy tale language this goal is spoken of as "the marriage with the Princess, whose beauty dazzles like the sun rising from the sea." Such a path is a quest and a quest involves many questions. A spiritual path cannot exist without questioning. Ivan knows of Princess Vasilissa, but he needs to find her and to win her hand. Through Prince Ivan's quest, the reader is invited to experience the questions, the marvels, the trials and tribulations of a soul's journey.

When Prince Ivan set out on his path, he shows faithfulness as well as persistence in the pursuit of his goal. He accepts the advice of the ants, the fish, and the ravens, each of which encouraged him not to give up when his strength failed and doubt prevailed. Ivan's greatest reward, however, comes to him when the Firebird appears. The Firebird, just like the king, knows Princess Vasilissa in her innermost being. He even uses the same words to describe her and is able to reveal to the prince her whereabouts.

Prince Ivan has golden arms up to his elbows and silver legs up to his knees. He also has a forehead that is both golden and silver, according to the time of day. These are very strange images, if taken literally. According to anthroposophy, moon forces are connected with humanity's past and sun forces with the future. In the fairy tale this connection to the sun and moon is represented by Ivan's forehead, which turns golden during the day, when the sun shines, and silver at night, when the moon is out.

And what does one make of Prince Ivan's silver legs and golden arms? When a human being incarnates, he brings with him his karmic past to work on. He is bound to the earth through his legs. The past is connected to the moon forces and depicted through the color silver. His arms are free, and his hands can easily stretch upwards to the heavens and to the sun, bringing about the possibility for creative work for the future.

Throughout history, the being of the Christ appears in different cultures as the God of the Sun. According to Rudolf Steiner, "until the Mystery of Golgotha, Christ's dwelling-place was the sun."[11]

The Secret of Numbers

In this beautiful description of Prince Ivan's physical body, the fairy tale indicates that he unites within himself the evolution of mankind, its past and its future. Further, it is told that as a child Prince Ivan slept for nine years. In fact the text is quite specific as to the length of Prince Ivan's sleep: nine years, nine months, nine weeks and nine days.

Lionel Stebbing, an anthroposophical researcher, wrote, " 'Everything is number,' declared Plato. 'When God called the world into existence, He worked as a mathematician,' said Pythagoras. Number is the secret of things. Number rules everything; it is a weaving, living essence. For Pythagoras, nine was an emblem of matter that, though continually changing its form, is never annihilated. It was also consecrated to the spheres, because the circumference of a sphere is 360 degrees, and 3 and 6 and 0 are equal to 9."[12]

What does the number nine represent in this context? It is nine years, nine months, nine weeks, and nine days. There are different ways of understanding this, as each of these is a mystery regarding time. Nine months, for example, is the time during which a child is in his mother's womb. Here he is safe and protected by Hierarchical Beings. Each new life on earth begins with a cry as the baby is forced to separate from the spiritual world. It is also known that from a physiological point of view, a change occurs in a child's development at around the age of nine. Before nine, a child is open to everything in his surroundings, and his ability to judge good and evil has not yet developed.

In illustration 32 the sun shines on everything. The feeling that we are presented with is that of a child who is secure and happy, and who lives in a harmonious environment. The child needs to feel that the adult world can be trusted and be able to develop confidence in those around him.

Around the ninth year, the child begins to look out into the world, a world that is not perfect. A new relationship must be found between himself and that which he now begins to discover. This requires strength. In *The Firebird*, Prince Ivan's father determines the young prince's strength by weighing him and measuring his height and width, before allowing him to go out into the world.

In anthroposophical medicine this phenomenon of the ninth year is described by the Drs. Husemann and Wolff: "With the ninth or tenth year, a new epoch begins in the development of the child. It is at this time that the ego, whose forces have been penetrating the organism from the head until this time, is directly engaged, 'coupled into the metabolic system,' as Rudolf Steiner expressed it, and thus, connected now with the whole organism. Man's soul-spiritual being begins for the first time to penetrate the entire organism to a certain extent."[13]

32
A child of seven draws the all-embracing sun.

What the nine-year-old child experiences inwardly was brought to expression in illustration 33. In this drawing the black door is closed, while two light-filled windows are extended from the house. The house represents the child's own self. A boat carrying two people is pulled to the house and anchored. The moment has come when he chooses his own friends—not everyone is invited.

Illustration 34 was drawn by another nine-year-old child. It is an example of how good and evil, or darkness and light, can be experienced. The sun is shining on the left only. The result is an orange castle with light-filled windows, a joyful child depicted in the flag, a green tree and an animal on the grass. On the other side of the valley, there is a black castle with a black figure on a black flag, surrounded by a dark cloud. The tree has no leaves and there is no animal. The young artist has shown us the division between the forces of good and evil. This is a new developmental step on the child's path.

With regard to nine weeks, let us consider the time period of the foetus. These nine weeks extend from conception to the beginning of the third month. At this time the developing individual begins to take on a human appearance.[14] He is a little closer to becoming a recognizable member of the human race. In this unusual way the fairy tale shows clearly that after his sleep Prince Ivan is ready to go out on his own. He starts a new life with a newly-awakened consciousness.

33

Illustrations by nine-year-old children showing the nine-year-old change

34

Character Traits that Live within Us

On their journey, heroes often meet different animals or creatures. This is also the case with Prince Ivan. The ants, the fish, and the ravens are connected to different spheres or elements. The ants live on the earth, the fish belong to the water, and the ravens fly through the air. Out of compassion each one of them is saved from death and is thereby given new life. Prince Ivan's help is different in all three cases. In the case of the ants, for example, the threatening danger comes from the world outside of the anthill.

The ant is one of the oldest surviving creatures on the earth and its advice to "never turn back until you comes to the end of your journey" is quite justified.[15] One can so easily imagine modern man in the situation of the confused ants, running from morning to night, every activity burning to be accomplished. In the English language, the expression "rat race" exemplifies this. The result is often burn-out. In order to advance on the path of spiritual development, an aspiring student must not succumb to these tendencies. In the story the prince frees the ants from the burning bush, restoring order and direction in their lives.

The next creature on Prince Ivan's path is the fish floundering on the beach. The fish pleads with Prince Ivan to throw him back into the water—which he does. In the element of water, life forces express themselves most strongly. This is an indication of the prince's personal relationship

35
Fish and Anchor
Early Christian
Domitilla Catacombs

to the fish. Why is the fish on the beach and not in the water? In the Christian tradition, the fish is seen as a symbol for the Christ Being. Prince Ivan finds the fish on the beach, indicating that within himself he has not yet found a living relationship to the Christ. The fish is also the zodiacal sign for Pisces. The sun rose in the sign of Pisces when Christianity began to spread. On walls and tombstones of the catacombs in Rome, the fish appears as a picture for streaming, surging life.[16] *Fish and Anchor*, from the Domitilla Catacombs (illustration 35), is an example.

The letters for the Greek word for *fish*, I X Θ Y Σ (*ichthys*) is an acronym for Iesous, Christos, Theou, Yios, Sōtēr, which translates into English as "Jesus Christ, God's Son, and Savior." In illustrations 30 and 31 one can see that the zodiacal sign of Pisces is connected to man's feet. From these drawings one may assume that the fish is the foundation on which the human being stands. The fish is also found in Andrea del Verrocchio's fifteenth-century painting, *Tobias and the Angel* (illustration 36). Guided by the Archangel Raphael, Tobias is shown carrying the fish in his hand. In this way he is shown as a follower of Christ.[17] Unlike Tobias and his connection with the Christ, Prince Ivan is not yet ready to carry the fish. Therefore, the fish asks the prince to put him back into the water.

Prince Ivan not only helps the ants and the fish, but he also feeds the baby ravens that have been left by their parents. They have fallen out of their nest and are unable to feed themselves. In Norse mythology the ravens are messengers for Odin.[18] They represent the inspiration that every student on the path of initiation needs. They are seen as spirit messengers. Their flights to and fro are an imagination for taking and bringing inspiration to and from the spiritual world.

36
Tobias and the Angel
ca. 1480
Andrea del Verrocchio

The two young ravens also point to a stage on the path of development. In the ninth century, "the raven" was a stage of development known to occult teachers and initiates. During that stage the pupil still walked in darkness; he had not yet reached the spirit light.

In order for the prince to reach the stage of "the raven," he must first fulfill certain prerequisites. These prerequisites are the development of humility, gentleness of soul, agility in thought, inner balance, and the ability to wonder. All of these qualities are mysteriously hidden in one's imagination of a beautiful deer. Hence it is a deer that Prince Ivan must feed to the ravens.

The Firebird as an Imagination of the Will

The aspiring student learns to recognize the qualities that he needs to foster in himself in order to become worthy of approaching the angelic world. Recall the Pharaoh with the Horus Falcon hovering behind him in chapter 2. The bird as a messenger appears repeatedly in mythology and fairy tales.

The three creatures Prince Ivan meets on his quest offer him the advice necessary for his path. The most important help, however, he finds through the bird that is connected to fire. Fairy tales that speak about fire emphasize that it is a special element. In this story fire appears twice. In the imagination of the ants, fire has an earthly character—it burns and brings destruction. On the other hand fire has a spiritual reality. After completing each task, the Firebird goes through the fire and arises out of the ashes anew, stronger and more beautiful than before. The Firebird can be seen as a metaphor for the human will. Once awakened from sleep, the human will grows slowly in purity, strength, and selflessness. How are the will and fire related to each other? Without the will there is no spiritual training. When the will is strengthened and filled with enthusiasm, it is of a fiery spiritual nature.[19]

The Firebird is always ready to serve. The symbol of this readiness is the Firebird's feather that Prince Ivan waves above his head to summon help. When the human being has awakened his will, it can be called upon at all times.

Building a Bridge to the Supersensible World

In many fairy tales one reads that all tasks are to be done in a single day. This is, of course, not to be taken literally, nor are these tasks of a physical nature. They are soul struggles and arise in a sphere where time as we know it does not exist. Nevertheless, giving up on the spiritual path as a result of weakness of will or fear is described in the fairy tale as death. When this occurs on a human path, the counterforces may succeed in keeping the human being in the dark, depicted in the fairy tale by the knights who became victims of Kostchei.

The tasks that Kostchei gives to Prince Ivan seem insurmountable. The first task of felling the trees, removing them, and cutting them into logs brings sunlight into the forest. When this has been achieved and the ground is prepared, Prince Ivan must plant the wheat. Princess Vasilissa—one's higher self—bakes the pirozhki from these grains.[20] Prince Ivan's ability to call on the Firebird, his will, and accomplish the tasks given to him, are a metaphor for a student of the spirit who calls on his will when he is confronted by evil, and overcoming these challenges is beneficial for the student's spiritual development.

When one thinks of a dark forest, there is lack of vision. It can be compared to dense thinking into which order and clarity must be brought. This can only be achieved by penetrating the process of thinking with will-activity that can clear the head.[21] The result of such will-activity can be living and nourishing, like the grain that in the story was harvested from the area where the forest was cleared. During the fulfillment of the tasks, Prince Ivan goes to speak with Princess Vasilissa. Her closeness and love give him strength and inspiration, and once the first task has been completed, Ivan's will is strengthened considerably.

The second task Kostchei demands of Prince Ivan is to dig a hole 17 miles long and 17 miles wide and completely fill it with water so deep that galley ships can sail on it. Again, one can imagine the strength that is demanded of him. He must dig a huge hole. How exhausting and demanding! Of course without the Firebird, this task would be unattainable. For a pupil on the initiation path, the idea of such extensive digging means greater effort for further will training, while the large body of water represents increased life forces. These etheric forces become available to the pupil for working on himself and in the world.

As the body of water requested by Kostchei must be large and deep enough for galleys, so an occult student's own ship, as he moves forward on the spiritual path, must be firmly held on course. In *The Magic Flute* by Mozart, the main character Tamino moves forward on his path of initiation, with strength and determination in all his endeavors. The imagination of the firebird in this fairy tale is, for Mozart, the magic flute. Through our will and heightened consciousness, we build a bridge between the sense-perceptible world and the world of the spirit. Water is connected to the life forces of man and can be linked to the flexibility of thinking. In old age, as the life forces of a human being decrease, so does his ability to think.

Overcoming Evil

To complete the second task, Prince Ivan is to create a bridge across the water. Of course, Kostchei the Deathless, the representative of evil, asks for many little springs on the bridge, so that he himself may benefit from the life-giving water. He entices the human being to complete all the tasks for his own purposes.

How does Kostchei appear on the scene? The fairy tale describes a huge black cloud covering the face of the sun. He is indeed a force which tries to extinguish the light; he is a counterforce of the sun. His kingdom is black; even the light coming through the windows of the castle is dark and his black eyes blaze with hatred. He wants the beautiful Princess Vasilissa as his bride. One may say that this is the evil force that wants to conquer purity and beauty.

Kostchei gets his nourishment and strength from human blood. Spiritual Science connects blood with the human ego, with warmth and fire, and with the will forces. Rudolf Steiner stated:

> In a phenomenon such as blushing, where shifting of the blood takes place, we have the very simplest form of the influencing of the blood system by way of the ego experience. Likewise, when we become pale from anxiety and fear, we have transitory expressions of ego-experiences clearly manifested in the instrument of the ego. The way the ego feels in fear or shame is expressed through its instrument, the blood.[22]

Blossoming and fruiting apple trees on the bridge is one of Kostchei's requirements. But because they have pearls instead of living seeds in their cores, the apples on the trees are not alive. They are decorative only and therefore spiritually worthless. Kostchei feeds these apples to the Firebird in order to preserve the black egg hidden in the beautiful bird. This shows to the reader that the will can also serve evil. All selfish motivations arising from an impure soul feed the interests of the counterforces. An awakened will which is built on selfish motives is disastrous for humanity. The will can serve the general good only when it is selfless.

Relinquishing One's Will to the Hierarchy

The time comes when the student must relinquish his own will for a higher purpose. He stands at the gate of the deepest insight into the mysteries of human nature. Before he can reach the highest goal, he has to sacrifice his will, which means he overcomes his own egoistic motives. In the story this deed occurs when the Firebird brings the sword and gives it to Prince Ivan. The Firebird asks for his own death so that the black egg inside him can be cut in half. Prince Ivan fulfills the request after he recalls the advice given to him by the young ravens: "Never refuse the request of a friend."

By killing the Firebird and destroying the black egg, Prince Ivan destroys Kostchei and frees Princess Vasilissa. She becomes the reward for his sacrifice. Only through a sacrificial act can one free one's higher self and unite completely with it.

It is Prince Ivan's intention to marry Princess Vasilissa and this marriage can take place only if he becomes totally selfless. In this context the Orans position, shown in illustration 37, may be of interest. It shows a departing soul relinquishing its will to the Christ. It is a gesture of complete surrender and selflessness.

Sleeping infants can often be found lying on their backs with their arms raised in this same position. This shows openness to the Christ impulse. Giving up one's own will can be seen as the moment when the human being realizes that his will must be replaced by Divine Will.[23] In Christianity this complete selflessness is expressed in St. Paul's words: "Not I but the Christ in me." Prince Ivan reaches this stage when he cuts the egg in half and kills Kostchei.

37
Mother of God, praying in the Orans position
Mosaic
Sophia Cathedral, Kiev

38
The Temptation of St. Anthony from the *Isenheim Altarpiece*
(1515) Colmar, France
Matthias Grünewald

Prior to reaching this stage, Prince Ivan's failed attempt to bring death to Kostchei exposes him to the terrible nature and persistence of all the evil spirit beings that attempt to destroy man. Kostchei waves his hand and horrible monsters, giants, headless ogres, ugly witches, lizards, devils, and dragons suddenly appear. *The Temptation of St. Anthony*, in Matthias Grünewald's *Isenheim Altarpiece* (illustration 38), is an example of how an artist depicts such evil beings. St. Anthony is beseeched by all manner of ugly demons, yet he is self-composed and even smiles at what would normally be a terrifying experience.

After the defeat of Kostchei, the black kingdom becomes colorful and the whole castle is filled with light and movement. Prince Ivan has freed one hundred knights whom Kostchei had killed and who now come to life again. Prince Ivan marries Princess Vasilissa and the outcome is most sublime. The moment has arrived when the human being is able to unite with his higher self. Noble impulses begin to flow as healing water of life through mankind. The world takes on a new embracing light, bringing with it the possibility of a new beginning for all.

Each student of the spirit who succeeds on this long and arduous path affects a world change. Whenever a human being unites with his higher self, this union becomes a joyful celebration. This spiritual marriage between Prince Ivan and Princess Vasilissa, his higher self, is symbolic of his having achieved cosmic harmony, and therefore the hierarchies rejoice. This is confirmed in the fairy tale by the following: When the king saw the couple, he wept tears of happiness and so did her three mothers, three grandmothers, and nine brothers.

A Glimpse into the Future:
Humanity as the Tenth Hierarchy

When humanity reaches the end of physical development on planet Earth, incarnations as we now know them will come to an end and development will continue in the spiritual world. Present humanity will become the Tenth Hierarchy.[24]

This is a glimpse into a far distant future. In a miraculous way, the same truths that are encountered in Spiritual Science, known as anthroposophy, have inspired artists for centuries. Wherever true statements are expressed artistically, the hierarchies are drawn to their proximity. That is one reason some icons can heal those who seek spiritual help and why temples and churches in the past were known to be holy places and the abode of spiritual beings. Thus, the world of angels, along with the beings of the other hierarchies, can act, unseen by mankind, in a protective and healing way.

One such artistic truth is *The Cross of San Damiano* (illustration 39). This icon rests in the Basilica di Santa Chiara, in Assisi, Italy. In the top part of the crucifix are ten light-filled angelic beings, and it appears as if the Christ is welcoming the tenth who would be none other than the spiritualized human being. Here it is disclosed, the revelation of a mystery that in the past may have been known only to initiates. It was not openly spoken about, but nevertheless found its way into artistic expression as is shown here.

The fairy tale of *The Firebird* reveals a great truth—that each person's successful struggle to connect with the spirit world benefits all of mankind. Through the ego, the will can be awakened and with the will, thinking and feeling can be transformed by the human being. Thoughts can be consciously raised to embrace positive attitudes towards life and all beings in the world, and feelings can be awakened from their dreamlike sleep. All deeds consciously taken in hand can become ever more healing in today's suffering and needy world.

39
The crucifix which spoke to
St. Francis at San Damiano,
Basilica di Santa Chiara,
Assisi, Italy (from a replica)
12th c.

The Vision of Ezekiel
Raphael

4 The Fisher-Prince with the Silver Apple

The fairy tale of *The Firebird* depicts in colorful imaginations the awakening of Prince Ivan's will as he follows his path of initiation. He wisely heeds the advice of the ants and the fish to "never give up" or "let go" of his decision to find his Princess. Once he receives the feather from the Firebird, he learns to use his will consciously by summoning it whenever he needs it. With the help of the raven's advice to "never refuse the request of a friend," he breaks the black egg and succeeds in overcoming the evil Kostchei. Only then is he truly free to marry Princess Vasilissa, a metaphor for the union with his higher self.

The initiation path continues in the story of *The Fisher-Prince with the Silver Apple* when the Prince learns to harmonize his forces of thinking, feeling, and willing.

40
The Hero Gilgamesh
Assyrian
8th c. BC

41
Lamassu guardian figure
Khorsabad
ca. 713–706 BC

Is there a work of art that expresses a strongly developed will force, allowing the viewer at the same time to perceive harmony between thinking, feeling, and willing? Such a creation would have to depict a human being who displays a well-developed character with outer physical strength and great self-discipline. At Khorsabad, in northern Iraq, an eighth-century stone relief of the hero King Gilgamesh (illustration 40) portrays these exact qualities. In this work of art the observer is introduced to a human being who, through the development of his will, was able to consciously master the soul qualities of thinking and feeling. A closer study of the sculpted relief reveals the wisdom of its creator. Before introducing the fairy tale of *The Fisher-Prince with the Silver Apple*,[1] it is important to explore this work of art in greater detail.

It is generally accepted that thinking is connected to the head. Observe the precise order with which Gilgamesh's hair and beard are arranged. The ability to think logically and systematically is important for one who wants to expand his thinking in order to develop inspirational thought. True fairy tales cannot be conceived solely by the day-to-day thinking of the human mind. They are gifts from a higher realm. In the same way, some of the great works of art are also inspirations from the higher realm and connect the viewer with universal truths.

Illustration 18 in chapter 2 is an example of an artist's ability to show the moment of inspiration. The falcon Horus stands directly behind the king's head and, as the god's messenger, he inspires the king with messages from the spirit world. Speech that is directed with clarity and purpose is related to thinking. Knowing when to speak and when to be silent belongs to a higher spiritual path. The hero Gilgamesh gives one the impression that he speaks only when it is necessary.

Man's ability to feel is centered in the chest area. This is also the location of the rhythmically beating heart and the continuous expansion and contraction of the lungs. Human feelings can be overwhelming when tears, laughter and pain soar out of control. A closer look at the Gilgamesh relief reveals that it is the lion that is used as a metaphor for man's life of feeling. This is illustrated in the English language with the expression "lion-hearted." The king holds the lion firmly with his left hand, the hand located on the side of the heart, indicating that he has taken charge of his life of feeling.

The third human faculty is willing. It resides in the limbs and in the metabolic processes. Educator A.C. Harwood stated, "People of strong will almost invariably move their limbs with energy and decision. When they walk they leave their impression on the ground; when they talk, the movements of the jaw, which is the limb of the head, or of the accompanying arms betoken the same liveliness in the system of movement. …It is not, however, only the limbs which are the basis of will; the metabolism plays its part as well."[2]

For centuries the bull has been regarded as a metaphor for will and strength. The saying "like a bull in a china shop" means someone is acting willfully in a delicate situation. One might well say that within man resides the strength of a sleeping bull. A perfect example of this strength is shown in illustration 3 (chapter 1) of the Lascaux Cave painting. In a human being this strength becomes the awakened will force.

The strength of Gilgamesh, his will force, is expressed in the relief through his muscular legs and arms. His feet point to the right indicating the future. A king carries his sword in his right hand and marches forward with his right foot. Gilgamesh lives in the present as is seen in his conscious forward-facing gaze. It is interesting to note that at Dur-Sharrukin, where the stone relief of King Gilgamesh was found, forceful winged bulls flanked him on either side (illustration 41).

When the will is awakened in order to accomplish helpful deeds, it becomes a healing force. This healing force is represented by a serpent or a snake. In the relief, Gilgamesh holds a serpent firmly in his right hand. The serpent is a well-known symbol used by the medical profession either as a single serpent encircling a staff—the staff of Asclepius—or as two intertwined serpents forming the winged caduceus—the staff of Hermes, or Mercury. Both staffs are used by medical organizations worldwide as respected symbols for the healing profession. Although on the one hand the serpent represents forces of good, on the other hand an aspiring pupil on a spiritual path must learn to gain mastery over the dark forces also connected to the serpent.

The following story was told by the chief of a First Nation's people at a public gathering: While out riding his horse one day, the chief dismounted and as he touched the ground was suddenly bitten by a rattlesnake. He forced himself back up onto his horse and rode home knowing that the snake bite might be fatal. When he got home, he could feel the paralyzing effect of the venom in his leg. In the following days he refused any outside help but instead chose to fight for his life spiritually. It took him over a week to overcome the pain and paralyzing effect on his body. He pointed out that during this time he had fought with the king of the snakes and that as a result he was now immune to all snake bites. In anthroposophy the king of the snakes is considered as a representation of the group ego of serpents and snakes.[3]

The stone relief of the ancient initiate King Gilgamesh portrays his inner spiritual development and his outer physical strength. This represents complete control of thinking, feeling, and willing faculties. He represents a future goal for all of mankind. It is a difficult one to reach, for it requires a high level of individual development. A human being can achieve this harmonious balance of his or her soul faculties—thinking, feeling, and willing, but it requires a firm commitment to the trials and tribulations on a path of initiation. Such a path is revealed in the fairy tale of *The Fisher-Prince with the Silver Apple*.

The Fisher-Prince with the Silver Apple

Once upon a time it so happened that an old fisherman lay dying in his simple hut on the shore of a great sea. His young son watched over him. In a whisper the old fisherman said to his son, "My boy, I am so poor, I have nothing to leave you except this shriveled, brown apple core. Plant it on my grave and may it bring you good fortune." Afterwards the old fisherman died and was buried, and the Fisher-Boy planted the apple core on his grave as his father had whispered.

The sun was setting when the Fisher-Boy came back alone to the hut. He was hungry, and so he took his net and cast it into the sea. When he pulled it out, he found a fish of pure gold in it, shining like the sun.

The Golden Fish cried out to him, "Put me back into the sea, O Fisher-Boy!" The boy was hungry, but he thought the fish was too beautiful to eat, so he put it back into the sea. The Golden Fish lifted its head above the water and said, "Because you were merciful, O Fisher-Boy, you shall be rewarded. Whenever you need wise counsel, come to the sea at sunset and call me, and I will come." Then he sank and swam away.

The Fisher-Boy went back to the hut and ate dry bread for his supper. Next day the Fisher-Boy went to his father's grave to lay a sea-poppy on it. He found that the shriveled apple core had already grown a tall stem. The following day there were leaves on the stem, and on the third day he found a beautiful silver apple that gleamed like moonlight on water. He plucked the silver apple and carried it carefully back to the hut. Its beauty delighted him. It had a long brown stalk with two soft green leaves on it.

The Fisher-Boy wondered what he could do with the silver apple. He felt that it was too beautiful to eat, and he thought of giving it to someone he loved. His father was dead, and he was all alone in the world, so he decided to ask the Golden Fish who had promised him wise counsel.

At sunset he walked to the edge of the sea and called softly, "Golden Fish! Golden Fish!"

The Golden Fish came and lifted its head above the water asking, "What counsel do you need, O Fisher-Boy?

The Fisher-Boy showed him the silver apple and said, "What should I do with this silver apple?"

The Golden Fish replied, "Toss it gently into the sea when the sun has set, but remember to bring it back to the land at sunrise." Then he sank and swam away.

The Fisher-Boy waited until the sun had completely set and then tossed the silver apple lightly into the sea. As soon as it touched the water, it began to grow and grow until it had grown into a round silver boat. The long brown stalk had transformed into a mast and the two soft green leaves had grown into two silken sails. The Fisher-Boy stepped into the round silver boat and sailed away.

All night long he sailed, and when the sun began to rise, he found that he had come to a country that he had never seen before. He stepped ashore and as the sun rose, the silver boat began to shrink and shrink until once again it was a silver apple with a long brown stalk and two soft green leaves.

In the distance, the Fisher-Boy saw a city with red roofs and white towers. He walked along the shore towards it, carrying his silver apple in his hand. On the way he passed by a tall granite pillar with a gold chain, a silver chain, and a bronze chain hanging from it. He was puzzled as to why the pillar was standing solitary on the flat deserted beach, away from ships and dwellings.

When he reached the city, he passed through a gate and came to a market place with many people. They were not buying and selling, nor shouting and jostling one another. There was no laughter or clapping each other on the back, as people do in market places. They were all dressed in black and standing silently or moving about slowly. Most were looking sadly at the ground.

Then one man looked up as the Fisher-Boy approached and when he saw him, he shouted with joy, "The Prince with the Silver Apple has come at last!" Others looked up and joined in the shouting until the whole market place was vibrating with the glad tidings. They continued with this shout as they carried the Fisher-Boy to the King's palace gates, where the Fisher-Boy was received with the same joyous welcome. He was quickly taken into the castle, along marble corridors of many colors until finally he was ushered into the throne room.

Inside the room it was very quiet. The only sound was that of stifled weeping. There were two thrones. On one of them sat the King in his magnificent crown and royal robes. He leaned his head wearily on his hand and his face showed grief and great pain. On the other throne sat the queen who was richly attired. Her eyes were closed and tears were falling freely. Her hand kept stroking the bright, unbound hair of a maiden who knelt before her. She was wearing a delicate robe made of peach-blossom and a girdle of amethysts. Her face was buried in the queen's lap, and her shoulders were shaking with sobs.

The King sighed deeply, before he turned round to see who had entered the throne room. When he saw the Fisher-Boy, he stared at him in silence for a moment. Was this a dream? Then he jumped up and cried out with joy, "Weep no more, dearest daughter! The Prince with the Silver Apple has come at last!" And he stepped down from his throne and embraced the Fisher-Boy, and drew him towards the queen.

"Sire, I am no Prince," the Fisher-Boy told him. "I am only a poor Fisher-Boy."

But the King replied, "Then I now proclaim you a Prince, and you shall be called the Fisher-Prince with the Silver Apple. Look up, my daughter, and welcome your deliverer." Then the Princess lifted her face as beautiful as the morning, and she and the Queen dried each other's tears. The Fisher-Prince with the Silver Apple was welcomed warmly and with joy.

The Fisher-Prince turned to the King and said, "Sire, tell me the cause of your sorrow, and why you and the people speak of my coming in this way?"

The King answered, "Once I had twelve daughters, all true and good and beautiful. Only one is left. She is the youngest and the one most loved. A fearsome dragon comes up out of the sea once every year and will destroy my entire kingdom if a king's daughter is not sacrificed to him. He has taken all my other daughters, and now the day draws near when my last one is to be taken. My wise men told me that only the Prince with the Silver Apple could save her. Now you have come."

The Fisher-Prince looked at the Princess and loved her. He said to the King, "Gladly will I give my life for her, but how can I fight such a dragon? All my life I have only cast nets into the sea."

"You must be armed with a sword of heavenly iron," replied the King. "The heavenly iron you must find yourself, and the sword you must shape yourself."

"How can I shape such a sword?" asked the Fisher-Prince, "I who have all my life only cast nets into the sea?"

The King answered, "The Heavenly Knight will teach you, in the Kingdom of the Stars."

Then the King had the Fisher-Boy with the Silver Apple dressed in clothes fit for a Prince. He gave him strange and precious gifts: a golden dagger, a drinking cup made of opal, a crystal thistle flower, and the skull of an elfin horse.

At sunset the Fisher-Prince with the Silver Apple went forth from the city and down to the edge of the sea, and he called softly to the Golden Fish, "Golden Fish! Golden Fish!"

The Golden Fish came, lifted his head above the water and asked, "What counsel do you need, O Fisher-Prince?"

Then the Fisher-Prince told the Golden Fish the story of the Princess and asked where he might find the heavenly iron with which to make the sword to fight the dragon. "You must sail in search of a shooting star," the Golden Fish told him, "but on your journey remember, whatever helpless creature you may meet, be to it as merciful as you were to me." Then he sank and swam away.

When the sun had set, the Fisher-Prince said farewell to the King, the Queen, and the Princess and gently tossed the silver apple into the sea. It grew once more into a round silver boat with green silken sails. And when he stepped into the boat, it sailed away.

In a short while he came to an island. It was all one big green meadow, and in the meadow a little blood-red calf was running to and fro, and it was weeping. "Why do you weep, little calf?" the Fisher-Prince called out.

The blood-red calf replied, "They have taken away my mother. And now I am all alone in the world."

The Fisher-Prince was sorry for the little calf, so he said, "Come with me, and I will take care of you." So he took the blood-red calf into the silver boat and they sailed on until they arrived at another island. It was all one big, dense jungle, and at the edge of the jungle lay a fire-colored lion-cub, weeping, with its head on its outstretched paws.

"Why do you weep, little lion-cub?" the Fisher-Prince called out.

The lion-cub lifted its head and replied, "My mother is trapped in a pit. And now I am all alone in the world."

The Fisher-Prince was sorry for the lion-cub, so he said, "Come with me, and I will take care of you." He took the fire-colored lion-cub into the silver boat and they sailed on until they came to a tall rock towering above the waves. In an eagle's nest on the top of the tall rock, a grey-feathered fledgling flapped its wings, and it was weeping.

"Why do you weep, little eagle?" the Fisher-Prince called out.

"My mother broke her wing and fell into the sea. Now I am all alone in the world."

The Fisher-Prince was sorry for the fledgling, so he said, "Come with me, and I will take care of you." So he took the grey-feathered fledgling into the silver boat, and they sailed on until they came to where the sky was full of shooting stars, as thick as sparks flying from an anvil. And just as they came to land at daybreak, one shooting star rushed past them, very close, and fell to earth with a thunderous sound, and there was great heat and a glow.

As soon as the boat had turned back into an apple, the Fisher-Prince went in search of the shooting star. He expected to find it still a star and still twinkling. But instead he found a deep crater in the earth, with the grass scorched around its edges, and at the bottom of the crater a hot, black, jagged, heavy stone.

The Fisher-Prince grasped the stone and returned to his three companions. But now they were cub and calf and fledgling no longer as they had been when he left them. During the time he had been away, looking for the shooting star, his three companions had been growing and growing until now they were fully-grown.

And now they no longer played pleasantly together. Instead they were fighting with each other. The Fisher-Prince separated them, calmed them, and made peace between them. And when the sun had set, the silver apple grew again into a round boat on the water, and they all set sail once more. As soon as the shooting star was taken into the boat, it turned into clear white light, and it was no longer a black, jagged, heavy stone but was shaped more like a hand. So the Fisher-Prince steered all night where the shining finger of light pointed, and at dawn they reached the Kingdom of the Stars.

Only a short distance from the shore they could see a bright fire burning. A sound of rhythmic clanging came from beside the fire, and with every clang there was a burst of shooting stars. With his silver apple in one hand and his shooting star in the other, and with his blood-red bull, his fire-colored lion, and his grey-feathered eagle beside him, the Fisher-Prince made his way to the fire. As he drew nearer, he saw that it was a forge, and he could see the Heavenly Knight tempering his great sword on the anvil.

The Heavenly Knight was clad in shining armor, with a cross and seven roses on his breast. His frame was that of a hero, and his strength was that of a hero, but when he turned his head to greet the Fisher-Prince, his countenance was that of a young boy. "What are you seeking from me, O Fisher-Prince?" he asked.

The Fisher-Prince told the Heavenly Knight the story of the Princess and begged to be taught how to shape a sword with which he might fight the dragon.

"Have you found the heavenly iron?" inquired the Heavenly Knight.

The Fisher-Prince stepped forward to show him his shooting star. And as soon as the bull and the lion and the eagle no longer felt the Fisher-Prince's gaze upon them, commanding them to be at peace with each other, they fell to squabbling again.

Then the Heavenly Knight said sternly to the Fisher-Prince, "I cannot teach you to shape a sword while you have such unmanageable companions. Come back to me when you have instead a golden eagle, a leaf-green bull, and a lion with a snow-white rose for a heart, who live together as brothers. Then will I gladly teach you."

So the Fisher-Prince sadly went back to the shore and with him his three companions, who were no longer quarrelling, but feeling very sorrowful because of the harm they had done him. At sunset the Fisher-Prince went to the edge of the sea and called softly, "Golden Fish! Golden Fish!"

And the Golden Fish came swimming and lifted his head above the water. "What counsel do you need, O Fisher-Prince?" The Fisher-Prince told the Golden Fish what the Heavenly Knight had said and asked how he could find the golden eagle, the leaf-green bull, and the lion with a snow-white rose for a heart.

"First," the Golden Fish told him, "you will have to find the Water of Life, the Sap of the Sun, and the Seed of the Dagger. These you can find only with the help of those who have returned evil for your good and now would redeem the evil." Then it sank and swam away.

The blood-red bull and the fire-colored lion and the grey-feathered eagle all felt repentant, and they came humbly to the Fisher-Prince, and begged him to let them help him. "Are you willing, then," he asked them, "that I should send you away and take instead as companions a golden eagle, a leaf-green bull, and a lion with a snow-white rose for a heart, as the Heavenly Knight directed?"

At the thought of leaving him, their hearts were heavy. Nevertheless they answered, "If that is the only way of redeeming the evil we have done you, then we are willing."

Then the Fisher-Prince asked his three companions, "Do you know where I can find the Water of Life?"

The eagle said, "I know. You must travel across all the four Kingdoms of the Clouds. Beyond the fourth Kingdom is the Kingdom of Chaos. And the Kingdom of Chaos is filled with the Water of Life."

"How can I get there?" asked the Fisher-Prince.

"I will take you there," answered the eagle.

So the eagle took the Fisher-Prince between his great, strong, grey-feathered wings, and they began to soar in wide, ascending spirals, upward, ever upward through the high blue air, in mighty, sweeping curves.

Presently, they came to the first Kingdom of the Clouds, a cold country where it was always twilight, so dark was the air of heavy mist. They flew upwards through this and came to the second Kingdom of Clouds. It was a country low and flat, and full of glowing colors. Still upward they flew through this to the third Kingdom of the Clouds, a warmer country of bright, white, airy mountain ranges. And upward still through this they flew until they came to the fourth Kingdom of the Clouds, where beautiful islands drifted like feathers in an ocean of warm light.

At last they arrived at the Kingdom of Chaos, a country so flaming with light that the Fisher-Prince was blinded by its radiance, though the eagle looked on it with steady eyes. Everywhere, in streams and rivers and seas of dazzling fire, ran the Water of Life. And the Fisher-Prince took out of his bosom the drinking-cup made out of opal that the King had given him, and he filled it with the radiant water. Then the eagle, with the Fisher-Prince, flew back through the four Cloud Kingdoms to where the fire-colored lion and the blood-red bull awaited them.

The Fisher-Prince then asked his three companions if they knew where he could find the Seed of the Dagger.

"I know," answered the bull. "You must plough the earth where green grass is growing with the golden dagger which the King gave you. And where you have ploughed, wheat will grow, which sings and which shines like a candle. When it has begun to sing and shine, you must pluck it. And that is the Seed of the Dagger."

"How shall I plough the earth with the golden dagger?" asked the Fisher-Prince.

The bull replied, "You must harness me to it with ropes of ivy and strands of honeysuckle, and we will plough together."

So the Fisher-Prince found a place where green grass grew. He took the golden dagger from his belt and harnessed the bull to it with ropes of ivy and strands of honeysuckle. And they ploughed the earth together. Wheat sprang up from the ploughed earth, and it began to sing and to shine like a candle. The Fisher-Prince plucked the ears of singing, shining wheat. Then he took from his pouch of purple leather the skull of the elfin horse that the King had given him, and into it he placed the wheat that was the Seed of the Dagger.

Then the Fisher-Prince asked his three companions if they knew where to find the Sap of the Sun. "I know," answered the lion. "You must clear a space in the jungle and purify it of all poisonous plants. A vine will spring up there and grapes will grow on the vine, and the grapes will begin to glow with a light like that of a ruby. When they begin to glow, you must pluck them and crush them, and a juice like purple sunlight will flow from them. And that is the Sap of the Sun."

"How shall I purify the jungle of all poisonous plants?" asked the Fisher-Prince. And the lion replied, "I will show you when we get there."

Then the lion led the way to the jungle, and it was an evil and foul-smelling place. And they cleared a space in it. Then the lion ripped open his side with his claws and tore out his heart, and laid it on the ground. Immediately, all the poisonous plants withered and died and the evil stench disappeared. In its place a sweet fragrance, like that of roses, filled the air.

Out of the lion's heart there sprang a vine. Grapes grew on the vine and the grapes began to glow with a light like that of a ruby. The Fisher-Prince then plucked the grapes and crushed them between his palms. From this the Sap of the Sun flowed out like purple sunlight. Then he took from his red velvet cap the crystal thistle-flower, which the King had given him, and in this he caught the flowing Sap of the Sun.

At sunset the Fisher-Prince went once again to the edge of the sea and called softly, "Golden Fish, Golden Fish!"

The Golden Fish came, and lifted its head above the water and asked, "What counsel do you need, O Fisher-Prince?"

"I have found the Water of Life and the Sap of the Sun and the Seed of the Dagger," said the Fisher-Prince. "What must I do now, O Golden Fish?"

The Golden Fish replied, "Give the Seed of the Dagger to the grey-feathered eagle. Give the Water of Life to the fire-colored lion. Give the Sap of the Sun to the blood-red bull." Then he sank and swam away.

So the Fisher-Prince took the skull of the elfin horse, which held the Seed of the Dagger, and brought it to the eagle. The eagle ate the Seed of the Dagger. Immediately his grey wings turned into golden ones.

Then the Fisher-Prince took the drinking cup made out of opal, which held the Water of Life, and brought it to the lion. The lion drank the Water of Life. Immediately a snow-white rose grew where his heart had been.

Next the Fisher-Prince took the crystal thistle-flower that held the Sap of the Sun and brought it to the bull. The bull drank the Sap of the Sun. Immediately his blood-red hide turned to the living green of leaves.

Now the Fisher-Prince was ready to go back to the Heavenly Knight, and with him travelled the golden eagle and the leaf-green bull and the lion with a snow-white rose for a heart. When the Heavenly Knight saw them, he rejoiced and said, "The eagle gained the Water of Life for the lion with his flight; the bull gained the Seed of the Dagger for the eagle with his labor; the lion gained the Sap of the Sun for the bull with his sacrifice. So have they served one another, becoming brothers, and henceforth can they live together in peace. Now, O Fisher-Prince, I can teach you how to shape a sword of heavenly iron."

So the shooting star that the Fisher-Prince had brought was heated at the forge and laid upon the anvil. And the Heavenly Knight taught the Fisher-Prince how to shape it into a keen sword, while the golden eagle and the leaf-green bull and the lion with a snow-white rose for a heart looked on in great content. In a short while the sword lay cold upon the anvil—like a cross of light. Then the Heavenly Knight buckled the sword in its belt about the waist of the Fisher-Prince, and bade him Godspeed in his fight against the dragon.

The Fisher-Prince thanked the Heavenly Knight for his help and came down to the sea with his three companions at the setting of the sun. The silver apple turned into the round boat as soon as it touched the water, and in it they sailed away from the Kingdom of the Stars. On the boat the sword of heavenly iron shone like a white flame, pointing the way to the country of the Princess.

At dawn they reached its shores and walked at the water's edge toward the city. As they drew near to the tall granite pillar, which stood apart on the sands, they saw against it a solitary drooping figure. They hurried and saw that it was the Princess in her robe made of peach-blossom with her girdle of amethysts. She was bound to the pillar with the chain of gold, the chain of silver, and the chain of bronze.

Then the Fisher-Prince drew his sword swiftly and tried to cleave the chains, but the Princess told him sadly, "Nothing in the world can cleave these chains except the dragon's breath."

The Fisher-Prince looked to the left and to the right, but he saw no one to help him in saving the Princess. But far away, in the distant mountains, from the red roofs and white towers of the city, throngs of people were watching breathlessly.

Suddenly the Fisher-Prince heard a loud roar behind him, sounding like many waters. He saw a gigantic wave approaching, churning and tossing the surface of the sea. Out of the wave rose a dragon which looked more fearsome than he had imagined. The dragon was covered in overlapping metal scales. Three rows of cruel spikes ran along his spine. His enormous tail thrashed to and fro like a heavy-toothed whip. From the cavern of his mouth, black smoke and orange flames came forth.

The dragon lumbered menacingly and triumphantly towards the Princess. The Princess moaned and shook her hair about her face to shield herself from the dreadful sight. Then the Fisher-Prince rushed between the dragon and the Princess with his sword held high, ready for combat.

A long and weary fight began because the dragon was many times bigger and more powerful than the Fisher-Prince. His sword of heavenly iron could not penetrate between the overlapping metal scales.

The fiery dragon's breath scorched him, his mighty tail scourged him, and the sharp and venomous talons created many bleeding wounds on his body. Slowly he began to weaken through the burns inflicted by the dragon and loss of blood. Faltering, he called out to his three companions, "Help me, my companions, or else I will fall and the Princess will perish!"

The golden eagle came and beat with his powerful wings at the dragon's eyes so that he could not see. The leaf-green bull pinned down the lashing tail with his strong horns, so that it could no longer scourge the Fisher-Prince. And the lion laid his mighty paw on the dragon's heart and held him firmly to the sand.

As the dragon opened his mouth to breathe forth fiercer flames, the Fisher-Prince, using the last of his strength, thrust the sword of light deep into it. The dragon lay spent and helpless, in a spreading pool of his own dark blood.

The Fisher-Prince was ready to kill the dragon, but the Princess called to him, "No, do not kill the dragon, because only through his breath can I be released from these three chains. Take my girdle of amethysts and put it around his neck. Lead him by it, and he will be tamed."

So the Fisher-Prince took the girdle of amethysts from the Princess and placed it about the dragon's neck. He then held one end in his hand and led the dragon by it.

The dragon came quite meekly and quietly to the tall granite pillar and breathed gently on the chain of gold, the chain of silver, and the chain of bronze. And they fell away as soon as his breath touched them, and the Princess was free.

Again the Fisher-Prince was ready to kill the dragon, and again the Princess restrained him. "No," she said. "The dragon must be conquered, but not killed, for it is his breath that warms the world. Men need the dragon's fire."

So the Fisher-Prince led the tamed dragon by the Princess's girdle of amethysts toward the city while the Princess rode upon the leaf-green bull. The lion with a snow-white rose for a heart walked beside the Princess, with her hand resting on his fire-colored mane. In the meantime, the golden eagle perched in a friendly manner on the head of the dragon, and the dragon welcomed him.

Everyone in the city came to meet them wearing their most beautiful clothes, singing and scattering flowers everywhere. The King and Queen, dressed in their crowns and royal garments, met them at the gates of the palace and kissed them and wept for joy. Then the Fisher-Prince with the Silver Apple was wedded to the Princess, and they lived happily in the palace with the King and Queen.

As for the golden eagle, the leaf-green bull, and the lion with a snow-white rose for a heart, they ate from their plates and slept in their bedchamber. Meanwhile, the dragon, with the Princess's girdle of amethysts about his neck, wandered through the palace gardens, harming no one and gently warming the world with his fiery breath.

Rudolf Steiner suggested the following opening and closing statements for a fairy tale, "Once upon a time it happened—now where was it? Well, where then exactly did it not happen?"[4] Such an opening statement evokes one's imagination and connects the fairy tale to the higher world. For a closing statement Steiner suggested, "I once saw this, and if what happened in the spiritual world did not succumb to death, if it is not dead, it must still be alive today." Again in the words of Rudolf Steiner, "That is precisely the way in which every fairy tale should be related. The proper atmosphere is created if the fairy tale always begins and ends in this manner."[5]

What are the mysteries that lie hidden in *The Fisher-Prince with the Silver Apple* that will enrich one's experience of the fairy tale?

The son and his father live by the sea, not in a forest or in a field. In this fairy tale the proximity of the ocean to the hut is important as it places the Fisher-Boy close to the environment from which later the Golden Fish surfaces. This setting, close to the element of water and the Golden Fish, points the reader to the life-giving forces of water. Through the loss of his father, the boy leaves his childhood behind and enters the independence of adulthood. He has to enter the future through his own efforts and in doing so, he becomes conscious of himself, discovers the world and makes new connections.[6]

Does the shriveled apple core have any importance in this fairy tale? He must plant and nurture it. A new apple tree grows quickly and he plucks from it a silver apple. Then he is told by the fish to "toss the apple gently into the sea when the sun has set and bring it back to the land at sunrise."

The Moon and Silver

Why a silver apple, when to us an apple is most appealing when it has a healthy red or yellow color? In his book, *Planets and Metals*, Kollerstrom states that silver and the moon have always been connected. Traditionally, the silvery moon was associated with the chaste goddess Artemis, the huntress with the silver bow. Curiously the fish suggests that the Fisher Boy toss his apple into the ocean at sunset, at a time when the moon comes to the fore. This is the time when the human being prepares for the night. And he is to bring it back to land at sunrise. The moon has the ability to reflect sunlight; it does not have its own light. The metal silver was used when a reflected quality was needed. When man thinks, it is either connected to one's intellect or it is inspired by higher beings. At night, however, when sleep occurs, one has to let go of both forms of thinking. One can envision that what man has done and thought is reflected during sleep. The imagination of a boat carrying the "sleeper" to other lands is beautiful. It describes what really happens. In the fifth volume of *Karmic Relationships*, Rudolf Steiner speaks about primeval teachers of humanity whose task it is to reflect and record man's thoughts and deeds as his being passes through the moon sphere. Rudolf Steiner stated: "Everything is observed and inscribed into the Akasha substance, as living reality, not in the form of an abstract script. These spiritual Moon Beings, who were the great Teachers during the age of primeval cosmic wisdom, are the recorders of the experiences of mankind. …

Everything they have preserved is engraved into his astral body."[7] Whatever lives at night slowly makes its way into our daytime consciousness, just as it happens to the Fisher-Prince.

Mankind's Return to the Spiritual World

All of the following images—the ocean, the father and his boy entering adulthood as a "fisher man," or leader, and the apple core growing into a tree with a silver apple—can be compared to the Old Testament story in Genesis. This story of Adam and Eve depicts man's origin in Paradise and his expulsion to Earth. Had man remained in Paradise under the protection and care of the Father, he would never have been able to achieve self-consciousness or independence and freedom. This freedom which he was given, allowed man to choose between good and evil. It gave him the ability to err, as well as the capacity to rise above evil through his own strength. A return to the heavenly kingdom was made possible. It is this epic struggle that is revealed in *The Fisher-Prince with the Silver Apple*. Prince Ivan takes his spiritual development into his own hands, and so too does the Fisher-Prince. The Fisher-Boy searches for his Princess, the Kingdom of the Stars and the Heavenly Knight. These are experiences of his higher self (the Princess), the world of hierarchical beings (the Kingdom of the Stars), and the spiritual guidance he received (the Heavenly Knight.)

At the present stage of human evolution, a quest for spiritual truths is very important. Only insight into spiritual realities that provide a true understanding of our planet and its place in the cosmos can help save it from destruction. Human beings have become co-creators and need the protection and inspiration of the hierarchical world. Only through individual efforts can such steps be made.

In illustration 27 (*Isenheim Altarpiece*), chapter 3, black clouds hover over the Virgin. Could those possibly depict humanity's lack of striving to connect with the spiritual world? In the painting, light is shown streaming down from the heavens to the pure soul, the Virgin.

There have always been two distinct paths of evolution for mankind that connect humanity to the spiritual world. Rudolf Steiner describes these two paths in the Temple Legend.[8] One path, depicted biblically as that of Cain, requires that man offer to the spiritual world fruit from the earth, gained through his own labor. On the other path, that of Abel, man is graced by benevolent hierarchies to receive inspiration—knowledge, ideas and wisdom—which he then has to digest and transform for his existence on earth. In this fairy tale, the first path is represented by the apple seeds planted over the father's grave, the second by the shooting star—inspiration from the cosmos. It is the first path, the path of offering of the fruit of the earth that the Fisher-Boy embarks upon.

The apple which can be connected symbolically to the Tree of Knowledge of Good and Evil is first received by the boy from his ancestor in the form of an apple core. Planted over his father's grave, the core produces a new tree on which ripens a silver apple. As indicated in the story of *The Firebird*, silver connects us to the past and contains the qualities and capacities developed during past incarnations.[9]

In the story of the Fisher-Prince, when the silver apple is tossed into the sea at sunset, it transforms into a boat. This is a metaphor for humanity's nightly journey during sleep into the kingdom of the stars. Here, together with guiding spiritual beings, the previous day is reviewed. While sailing in the spiritual ocean, man's consciousness is indeed in another country. When asleep, man's connection to the spiritual world and its life forces restores depleted strength. A person who is exhausted before sleep feels comforted, enlivened, and refreshed upon awakening.[10]

The Fisher-Prince and his companions experience the spiritual world during the night. In reality, everything that occurs nightly to a person slowly enters the consciousness of his waking life and is worked upon with his soul during the day. The boat with the silken sails reverts into a silver apple each morning and its spiritual encounters and revitalizing possibilities are hidden from daytime consciousness. The Fisher-Boy begins his journey with a search for truth. On the one hand, he needs to go forward through his own efforts; on the other, he is dependent on the help and advice of others. This help and advice is given only when he asks a question. The response comes to him from three different sources. One source is the Golden Fish. The fish, as mentioned earlier, is a symbol for the Christ. Help also comes from the Heavenly Knight, who can be compared to the great Archangel Michael, depicted throughout the ages as man's helper in the fight against the dragon. It is the Heavenly Knight who forges the sword (the third source) out of meteoric iron, but only after all the necessary work has been accomplished by the Fisher-Prince and his companions.

In Every Human Being Lives a Prince

When the Fisher-Boy arrives in the marketplace of the King's city, he is recognized as a person of noble stature. Although he regards himself as a lowly Fisher-Boy, the King quickly proclaims him to be a Prince and gives him a new attire. May we assume that such a Prince lives within each of us even if we are not aware of it? The human being must be humble, but at the same time an individual must know that he has within himself the strength and the ability to become a true Prince. To recognize someone as a Prince means to acknowledge him as the son of the King. The King in this context can be seen as God. Seeds placed in the human being during creation by the Divine must now grow and bear fruit in honor of our Divine origin. Every striving individual can become worthy by developing his spiritual potential. The King recognizes in the Fisher-Boy such a striving individual.

In the opening words of the Gospel according to John, Christ gives the power to those who receive Him, to become the Sons of God.[11] This points to a potentially sublime future for mankind.

As with Prince Ivan in *The Firebird*, the Fisher-Prince represents every individual on earth and his story can therefore speak to everyone. Through this fairy tale we are shown that the Divinity expects that mankind's evolution be taken up by human beings themselves, regardless of race or religion. This is a prerequisite if our Earth is to become the planet of love and freedom.[12]

Freeing a princess from a dragon and winning her hand is the ultimate goal in many fairy tales. In this fairy tale, eleven of the King's daughters are sacrificed to the dragon—only one remains. Hope rests alone on the Fisher-Prince to rescue the twelfth. It will be the last chance for the future of the kingdom.

How does one relate to the fact that the King has twelve daughters, and that all were devoured by the dragon except for one? The reader must remain flexible in his thinking and guard against fixing images to one interpretation only. In the previous chapter the Princess has been seen as an image for the higher self of a human being. However, imaginations are living pictures. Could it be that in this story attributes of the human soul are addressed as the twelve sisters? One might think of the sisters as the following virtues: devotion, equilibrium, perseverance, selflessness, compassion, courtesy, contentment, patience, control of speech, courage, discretion and magnanimity.[13]

The seeds for these virtues are laid at birth into a human soul. Insight and strength derived from anthroposophy can help adults raise their children in such a way that such seeds are nurtured. In addition, when these virtues are practiced, they become a source of strength beneficial to one's ability to cope with everyday life.

Every human being is responsible for society's spiritual health, or the lack of it. Rudolf Steiner spoke about the twelve virtues in a very special way and connects them to the twelve signs of the zodiac, each with its own transformative potential.[14] Could these be powers and capacities that will guide the human being on his path into the future and give him strength to survive?

The Blood-Red Calf, the Fire-Colored Lion-Cub, and the Fledgling Eagle

With the help of the Golden Fish, the Fisher-Prince develops his virtues. Becoming compassionate and taking all helpless creatures into his care are pieces of advice he is given. Who are these creatures and what do they represent?

The Fisher-Prince meets the creatures on his soul's journey. Within him lives what he discovers to be a blood-red calf, representing a force that when awakened can manifest as a bull. It can become an unrestrained, ungovernable will energy, which would need to be tamed.

The Fisher-Prince is asked to return to the Heavenly Knight with a tamed, leaf-green bull, representing the transformed will energy. Green is the color of life-imbued nature with which we associate growth. It brings balance to the soul. According to Spiritual Science all the planets are connected to colors. Mars is red. When one finds Mars in the sky, it can be seen as a reddish star. It is no coincidence that this planet is connected to the will force. In Roman mythology Mars is the God of War, as well as the God of Agriculture, the force which transforms the earth.

The fire-colored lion-cub, although still young and dreamy, has an emotional feeling life which harbors an uncontrolled temper. It too is tamed through the self-sacrificing of his own heart for the good of others.

Everyone experiences diverse and often scattered and uncontrolled thoughts, represented in this story as an eagle fledgling with grey wings. The eaglet bravely carries the Fisher-Prince into the Kingdom of Chaos, to fill the cup made of opal with the Water of Life.

All three creatures are still young and immature. They have to be guided as they grow. Their soul qualities must be cared for and transformed. As these animals in the story go through a transformation, so too, can the human being.

The Bull, the Lion, the Eagle, and the Angel in the Zodiac

A profound mystery is revealed to the reader of this story, namely that the eagle, the lion and the bull represent man's soul qualities of thinking, feeling and willing. These three creatures are connected not only with the soul of the human being, but also with the entire cosmos. This is reflected in the zodiacal signs.

Rudolf Steiner stated, "Our forefathers, still conscious of these important facts through tradition, represent the Cherubim as strangely winged beasts with variously shaped heads: The winged Lion, the winged Eagle, the winged Bull, and the winged Man."[15] Unlike the other three signs which are represented by beings connected to the animal kingdom, Aquarius is represented by an angelic being. This could be seen as the future angelic human being, who has developed a perfected balance of thinking, feeling, and willing. Such cosmic forces streaming down from highly evolved spiritual beings were once perceived by man while gazing up at the sky. These spiritual forces provided the seeds for man's capacities to think, feel and will harmoniously. Raphael's painting of *The Vision of Ezekiel* (illustration 42) portrays their powerful strength. Ezekiel points to the hierarchy connected to these four archetypes when he says, "As for the likeness of their faces, they four had the faces of a man and a lion on the right side, and they four had the face of an ox on the left side; they four also had the face of an eagle."[16]

42
The Vision of Ezekiel
Raphael (1483–1520)

This unusual description that emphasizes that "they four had the faces of…" reveals that they show their own faces but within each of them live the three others. In St. John's Book of Revelation it is written: "…And around about the throne, were four beasts, full of eyes before and behind. And the first beast was like a lion, and the second beast was like a calf, and the third beast had a face as a man, and the fourth beast was like a flying eagle."[17]

Rudolf Steiner refers to the connection of the cosmic beings, represented by these animals, with the human physical body. Man's physical body and psyche is connected to the macrocosm where the lion, the bull, and the eagle are manifest.[18]

43
The Son of Man, 12th c., Chartres Cathedral

In pre-Christian times as well as in the Christian culture, the three beasts are well-known symbols, precisely because in the human being they represent the capacities of thinking, feeling, and willing. Over the magnificent West Portal of Chartres Cathedral, in France (illustration 43), Christ is shown in His full glory surrounded by the four winged beings— the Eagle, the Lion, the Bull and the Angel. In the Christian tradition these four beings are also symbols for the four writers of the Gospels and the four soul attributes: John (thinking, eagle), Mark (feeling, lion), Luke (willing, bull), and Matthew (angel-man, balance), and depicted on the walls of many cathedrals and churches.

Anthroposophy refers to different initiation streams, which are inspired by spiritual beings and connected to different cultures. The following quotation is taken from Rudolf Steiner's *Gospel of Saint John*: "Thus you could find Mystery temples in Asia Minor, or in Egypt, where the initiation took a form that brought about the vision of the lofty spiritual beings as Bull spirits or as Eagle spirits. And it was in the Mysteries that outer culture had its source. …For everything we find in the way of outer cult usages among the different peoples, derived from the initiation rites. There were initiates everywhere whose spiritual vision was focused principally on the Bull spirits, others attuned primarily to the Eagle spirits, and so on. To a certain extent we can even indicate the differences in the various modes of initiation."[19]

The gospel writers of the New Testament stand before humanity as initiates from different spiritual streams. In the Christian tradition St. John is connected with the Eagle (illustration 44), St. Luke with the Bull (illustration 45), and St. Mark with the Lion (illustration 46). St. Matthew represented by an angel being is connected to Man (illustration 47). These examples are beautifully illustrated in the Irish manuscript, *The Book of Kells*, painted between the sixth and eighth centuries AD.

44

45

44–47
The Book of Kells, Plates 19, 49, 59 and 91
ca. AD 800

46

47

Harmonizing Thinking, Feeling, and Willing

When the Fisher-Prince arrives at the forge of the Heavenly Knight, he is not yet ready to receive the instruction for the shaping of his sword of cosmic iron. This is due to the fact that his three companions are still fighting amongst themselves. This signifies that as long as the soul qualities of thinking, feeling, and willing are not yet harmonized within an individual human being, there remains a lack of self-control and inner balance.

The quarrelling creatures in the fairy tale of the *Fisher-Prince* can be experienced by every human being in daily life. Such quarrels take place when one soul faculty dominates the others and balance is lost. One may say, for example, that a person who lives too strongly in his feelings may become a dreamy visionary, detached from the realities of life. An obsessive thinker who lives only in his thinking but is weak in his will capacity becomes pedantic and impractical. Also, a person who is too strongly attached to will forces and weak in thinking or feeling is in danger of overpowering and controlling others.

To achieve this control and balance is not an easy task. Thinking is at present the only fully conscious experience a human being can have. Rudolf Steiner pointed to the following: "In the true sense of the word, we are really awake only in our sense-perceptions and our life of ideas; in the life of feeling we are so near to sleeping as to be dreaming; and in the life of will we are always fast asleep."[20] In this respect, the relief of King Gilgamesh (illustration 40) can represent the soul forces of thinking, feeling, and willing in perfect balance.

Man recognized the importance of controlling and bringing the four archetypes into harmony long before the Christian era began. The Great Sphinx at Giza (illustration 48), which remains cloaked in mystery for many people, is one of the most powerful examples that exists today. When first built, the Sphinx is said to have had the wings of an eagle, the chest of a lion, and the hind of a bull. At the front of the body, a human head represents man's need to learn to live

48
The Great Sphinx, Giza, Egypt, 2530 BC

49
The Ecstasy of St. Cecilia
ca. 1516
Raphael

in balance with the innate forces of the bull, the emotions of the lion, and the thinking of the eagle. According to Steiner, "The features, which stand out separately in the Sphinx are in human nature inwardly interwoven."[21] Renaissance artist Raphael portrayed the three soul forces in the painting of *The Ecstasy of St. Cecilia* (illustration 49), with St. Paul and Mary Magdalene by her side. St. Paul, the strongest character in the painting, is on the left with his hand on his chin. He is wearing a red robe and a green top representing a controlled will. In the story of the Fisher-Prince the blood-red calf had to be transformed into a leaf-green bull. St. Paul's gaze is earthward. Is he contemplating the earth's transformation through the transformed will?

In the middle of the painting is St. Cecilia holding a musical instrument. She appears to be in a relaxed dreamy state as she gazes upward into the sky. Does she not give the impression that she represents all that which we feel? The third figure, the beautiful girl on the right, is very much awake as she looks straight into the world. She represents true thinking, which is calm, clear, and knowing. Her dress is reminiscent of flowing water, a metaphor for the process of thinking and its connection to the etheric body. Her forward-facing gaze is reflected in the fairy tale when the eagle, as representative of clear thinking, was able to look into the flaming light in the Kingdom of Chaos with steady eyes. Raphael connects the viewer to the source of these three attributes by leaving an opening in the clouds.

Ego Development and Shooting Stars

One of the main themes in fairy tales is the struggle for freedom. In the development of mankind, free will is something that humans may gradually acquire. The possibility of a free will is a constant ideal which can be attained only slowly in the course of time. As long as human beings are enmeshed in their lower instincts which manifest as hatred, desire, and strong emotions, they are subject to negative influences and therefore are not free. These influences which reside in the subconscious are not easily recognized nor easily overcome.

Freedom is one of the most important concepts in Christianity. The Christ connected Himself to the earth in order to assist the human being in this struggle. Through Christ, man can reconnect with the spiritual world and experience the spiritual within the ego. Meditating on an image of His cross can keep adversarial forces at bay. "Our earth development is designed to incorporate the ego into the being of man, so that man becomes a being fully self-conscious and capable of love and freedom. Thus the Earth can fulfill its mission of love."[22] Through self-knowledge that is received on the path of initiation, man slowly becomes more capable of dealing with weaknesses in thought, feeling and will. This path of initiation was well-known to the ancient Greeks. Engraved over the entrance to the ancient mystery temple of Apollo at Delphi is an inscription which reads, "Man Know Thyself."

The Fisher-Prince's final achievements on his journey lead to his ultimate freedom. This results in the freeing of the Princess from the dragon, the King and Queen from grief, and their people from fear. For this he had to find the heavenly iron and take it to the Heavenly Knight in the

Kingdom of the Stars. There he was taught how to forge and shape the sword. The fairy tale stresses that evil can be overcome only when the sword is forged and shaped by the one who owns it. It has to be made of heavenly iron, which in this story is the shooting star, an image of profound meaning. The shooting star on one hand can be regarded as an inspiration, which comes down from the heavens and connects the earth to the cosmos; on the other hand it can be seen as a heavenly messenger that disperses meteoric iron.

Rudolf Steiner made a connection between the shooting stars in the universe and the iron in our blood. "A man who looks out into space and sees a shooting star should say to himself, with reverence for the gods, 'That occurrence in the great expanse of space has its minute counterpart continuously in myself. There are the shooting stars, while in every one of my blood corpuscles iron is taking form: My life is full of shooting stars, miniature shooting stars.' "[23] The blood in turn is connected to the ego. It entered physically into man as a result of man's physical nature being endowed more and more with blood. "Our blood is the expression of our ego activity."[24]

To overcome the lack of control in thinking, feeling, and willing, it is important that man strengthen his ego forces. This assists him in his battle against evil. In the story, the sword represents the strengthened, pure ego which lives in inner uprightness in the human being. It now becomes clear why the sword must be shaped from heavenly iron and why evil can be fought only with such a sword.

Because the Fisher-Prince was not yet ready to reach out and receive inspired thoughts from the higher world, the shooting star is pictured as a jagged, heavy iron stone. The Prince, however, took it into his boat and carried it into the spiritual world where it was transformed into light that guided him in his further struggles and endeavors.

Transformation of the Soul Faculties: Thinking, Feeling, and Willing

On reaching the Heavenly Knight, the Fisher-Prince was given new tasks in order to help him reach a higher stage in his development. These tasks in fairy tale language were to find an eagle with golden wings, a leaf-green bull, and a lion with a snow-white rose for a heart. The Fisher-Prince puzzled over what to do and then asked the Golden Fish for advice. The Golden Fish answered, "First you must find the Water of Life, the Sap of the Sun, and the Seed of the Dagger." To achieve these tasks the Fisher-Prince makes use of the strange and precious gifts given to him by the King: the golden dagger, the crystal thistle flower, the drinking cup made of opal, and the skull of an elfin horse. The dagger is made of gold, the most noble and precious of all metals. Perhaps it is a reflection of the human being's connection to the spiritual sun. It is harnessed to the bull and used by the Fisher-Prince as a plow, an implement that prepares the earth for new growth and transformation. The will of the bull, needed to pull the golden dagger-plow, is a metaphor for the human will which has the potential to transform our planet, benefiting all. The other three gifts are vessels waiting to receive newly transformed human attributes. They symbolize gifts given to each soul at birth by God, and in this story, they were given to the Prince by the King.

Thinking

What is the meaning of the opal drinking cup? Opal is normally described as being either milky-colored or transparent. In the fairy tale one can assume that the transformation from a milky quality into a transparent vessel takes place when it is filled with the Water of Life. This is symbolic of dull thinking transformed into crystal clear thinking.

When one contemplates the skull of an elfin horse it is helpful to know that the image of a horse is connected to the human intellect. This is also the case for the Four Horsemen of the Apocalypse given as a revelation to St. John on Patmos. The apocalyptic revelation appears to him as four riders on different-colored horses. The first, a white horse, shows the power of useful intelligence. The second, a red horse, brings conflict and takes peace away from the earth. The third, a black horse, brings materialistic thought to the world; and the fourth, a pale horse, portrays the shadows of death.[25] In our time, humanity finds itself confronting the third black horse and is moving toward the fourth. If the laws of the material world continue to gain prevalence without man's developing spiritualized thinking, then destruction will occur.[26]

An elfin horse is weak, but swift. In the fairy tale, one can imagine that its skull is dainty, lifeless and empty and needs to be nourished with life-giving food from the Wheat of the Dagger. Human thoughts can also be dry and lifeless. However, they can be transformed into living and nourishing thoughts. Strong will forces are required for this strengthening of creative thinking.

Feeling

The crystal thistle flower is beautiful, but hard and prickly. It could be likened to our feelings which have the ability to stream forth uncontrollably and be hurtful to others. For its transformation, the crystal thistle flower needs to be filled with the Sap of the Sun, imbuing it with warmth and light.

From the beginning of the story the Fisher-Prince demonstrated the qualities of humility and sacrifice, prerequisites for any path of development. He regarded himself as a lowly Fisher-Boy, certainly not a Prince, and he willingly accepted advice. When hungry, he did not eat the Golden Fish because he felt compassion for it. He also wanted to give away the beautiful silver apple which grew on the tree over his father's grave.

For further development along the path of initiation, the Golden Fish makes the Prince aware of further qualities that he has to develop such as repentance and the willingness to redeem past wrongs. In the story, the Prince's animal companions show the need to redeem themselves because of their unruliness. They must be transformed, purified and balanced against one another. In the fairy tale the result is immediate. The three beasts are remorseful for having harmed the Fisher-Prince with their fighting, and they humbly beg that he allow them to help.

The eagle then offers to take the Fisher-Prince to the place of the Water of Life. He carries the Fisher-Prince through four different Kingdoms of the Clouds and on to the Kingdom of Chaos, where the Fisher-Prince is able to fill the cup made of opal with shining, living water.

50

Drawing by a ten-year-old child

The Fisher-Prince is faced with clouds and chaos, metaphors for different soul and physical conditions that can be encountered by the student on a path of initiation. Finally, earthly or intellectual thinking, which is connected to weight, measure, and number, becomes enlivened and enlightened. It transforms into creative spiritual thinking. The story with its picture imagery shows how closely thinking and feeling are connected.

For the third task, the Fisher-Prince has to find the Sap of the Sun and does so with the help of the lion, who also wants to redeem his past deeds. The lion, the archetypal symbol for the heart and our feeling life, leads the Prince to a jungle full of poisonous plants. The Prince then clears a place for the lion, who rips open his side and places his own heart on the ground. All the poisonous plants disappear and a vine grows from his heart. A human being can transform the earth through kind, sacrificial and sun-filled deeds. In the human being this happens when he begins to observe his own feelings and check his emotions.

When the Fisher-Prince crushes the grapes with his hands, purple juice flows from them. This is the Sap of the Sun, flowing like purple sunlight. Purple is the color of reverence and humility. If one surrounds oneself with purple in thought during meditation and does this many times, eventually the feeling of humility arises in the soul. A child uses the color purple freely, when humility and reverence live in his soul. This can be observed in a drawing by a ten-year-old girl (illustration 50). In this drawing a human being is sitting at a precipice catching a fish, while a black dog tries to attack. If one looks more closely, one sees a purple barrier between the dog, the tree, and the fisherman.

Willing

The Fisher-Prince has to then find the Seed of the Dagger. When he asks for help with this task, the bull comes to his aid, suggesting that with the golden dagger he plough the earth where the green grass is growing. Wheat will grow which sings and shines like a candle. This will be the Seed of the Dagger.

When the Fisher-Prince questions how this is to be done, the bull tells him to harness him with ropes of ivy and strands of honeysuckle. The human will needs continuous strengthening and harnessing and a pupil must hold it firmly in control. The ivy plant is very strong. Working on the will becomes a joy, which in the fairy tale is portrayed as the sweet scent of honeysuckle. What is the meaning of plowing the earth? In order to make growth possible, one needs to place one's efforts where they can bear fruit. When the will is consciously used for good deeds, a difference is made.

To consciously achieve control of his thinking, feeling, and willing, however, is not the final goal for man. In the fairy tale this is indicated through the sacrificial offering of the gifts, which the companions give to one another:

The eagle gave the Water of Life to the lion, whose heart, freed from egoistic feelings, was transformed into a Snow-White Rose. Only a pure heart is able to receive the Water of Life—which represents noble thoughts. It is spiritually-inspired, clear thinking that penetrates man's feeling life. This shows that an individual who is pure and performs sacrificial deeds, uses his heart forces when applying himself to the right causes.

The bull brought the Seed of the Dagger to the eagle, whose wings immediately turned golden. In a human being this indicates the capacity to persevere when seeking spiritual insight and truth. Thinking now becomes enlightened thinking.

The lion brought the Sap of the Sun to the bull, who immediately transformed into a green-leaf bull. This indicates that warmth can permeate controlled will forces, allowing an individual to create deeds filled with love.

The understanding of the story of the Fisher-Prince is not complete until the following is considered: When the Christ met the woman of Samaria at the well, He said, "But the water that I shall give him shall be in him a well of water springing up into everlasting life." He also spoke the following: "I am the true Vine"[27] and "I am the Bread of Life."[28]

In the story, the Lion says to the Fisher-Prince: "And grapes will grow on the vine, and the grapes will begin to glow with a light like that of a ruby. …And a juice like purple sunlight will

51

The Risen Christ
Graduale from St. Gallen
11th c.

flow from them. And that is the Sap of the Sun." The use of the colors as indicated in the fairy tale, are found in an eleventh-century icon of *The Risen Christ* (illustration 51). The vine was the first plant grown on the earth by Noah after the flood.[29] Spiritual Science connects the first use of wine with developing ego forces in humanity. Later, wine became misused and began to dim the ego consciousness.

In illustration 52, a young child drew unknowingly all the elements that contribute to life-giving forces: the true green of the vine, the ripeness of the fruit, the purple dress in a position of repose, and the light and warmth of the sun. It is also significant that the girdle of the Princess is made of amethysts and that the Fisher-Prince ties it around the neck of the dragon. The color of amethyst is purple or wine-colored. The word *amethyst* comes from the Greek *amethyein*, which means 'not being drunk,' or, in other words, 'of a clear consciousness.' In the picture of *The Risen Christ*, the vine's leaf-green and amethyst colors are connected to the gold-adorned image of Christ as He appears to be stepping forward.

The chains which bind the Princess to the granite pillar are made of gold, silver, and bronze. Bronze is an alloy consisting mainly of copper and tin. In Goethe's fairy tale *The Green Snake and the Beautiful Lily*, the three kings in the subterranean chamber are made of gold, silver, and bronze. Rudolf Steiner connects gold with knowledge and thinking, silver with feeling, and copper with the will.[30]

The chains which fall away from the Princess depict the resolution of obstacles that fetter the soul. Although the Fisher-Prince has already forged his own sword from meteoric iron and is able to conquer the dragon, he himself cannot free the Princess. Only the dragon is able to free the Princess from the chains with his fiery breath!

It is not enough to develop one's soul qualities. Without evil, there would be no freedom of choice. Evil forces like to work in the dark of man's unconscious nature. They normally tempt him and lead him astray. These forces cannot be totally vanquished; they can only be tamed. If the human being takes hold of these adversarial forces with the help of the Heavenly Knight and the Heavenly Sword, then evil forces can serve the good. This takes place through the strength of man's own ego, as well as with the help of heavenly beings.

In this story the dragon happily serves the kingdom, as evil can serve humanity once it has been overcome within an individual self. If human beings are indifferent or not conscious of evil, then out of this weakness evil will continue to be strengthened. To free the Princess from the dragon means to free one's own soul with the strength gained on the spiritual path of initiation. The fairy tale of *The Fisher-Prince with the Silver Apple* seems to dance like sunshine on water. It appears light and poetic, yet deeper insights reveal a remarkable description of a transformation of the soul faculties of thinking, feeling, and willing. In the future this will be required of every human being.

52
Drawing by an eleven-year-old child

Man with Light
Alexander Kharitinov

5   The Crystal Ball and the Silver Saucer

The stories of *The Firebird* and *The Fisher-Prince with the Silver Apple* bring the reader closer to an understanding of inspired fairy tales. While following the adventures of Prince Ivan and the Fisher-Prince, and their triumphs over challenges and obstacles, one becomes aware that these fairy tale heroes mirror what each human being may attain on his or her individual spiritual path. Two of the most important virtues that the heroes needed to develop were strength of character and expansion of consciousness. These led to the awakening and purification of the will and the acquisition of a harmonious interaction of the three soul forces: thinking, feeling and willing. Without the determination and endurance to reach his objectives and without expanding his consciousness while on the spiritual path, neither hero would have been able to reach his final goal of marriage to the Princess.

The stories, in spite of being described to the reader in fairy tale imagery, point to a universal truth: Any human being in our midst who has developed a pure and strong will and who harbors a peaceful inner life not only is a valuable individual to society but is also a developing leader of mankind.

The happy endings portrayed in fairy tales have always been accessible to seekers of the spirit. However, one must keep in mind that the spiritual transformations achieved in fairy tales are not likely to be reached in a short time in our own lives and will require steady and ongoing effort, even in subsequent incarnations.

When looking at the world around us, one may well ask, "How is it possible that mankind, guided as it is by the Hierarchies, has become so enmeshed in strife and destruction?" For the Earth to transform into "a planet of love and freedom," divine hierarchical beings require man's participation through the transformation of his consciousness. This can happen only if human beings embark on a spiritual path of study and acquire the ability to think spiritually. The spiritual objectives of the hierarchies remain firmly in place in spite of all the chaos that may unfold through world destiny.[1] Man has evolved to a new level of consciousness. Fully protected and guided by hierarchical beings during previous stages of incarnation, he needs to accept the fact that this new freedom given to him by spiritual hierarchies will be of benefit only if he develops ever greater responsibility towards himself, those around him, and the planet on which he lives.

53
Copy of
The Head of Christ,
detail from *The Last Supper*
1495–1497
Leonardo da Vinci

As discussed in the previous chapters, mankind has always been aided by exceptional individuals who were connected spiritually to the hierarchies and became their messengers, often through paintings, sculpture, music, and other forms of art. Their works have inspired countless souls to retain a connection with the spiritual world. Whose soul is not moved while listening to Beethoven's *Ninth Symphony* or gazing upon the face of Christ in Leonardo da Vinci's *The Last Supper* (illustration 53)?

Nordic and Greek mythologies, for example, speak of great evolutionary epochs that included all people and not simply individual souls. These sagas and epics were inspired by spiritual visions. They were understood by the initiates, who in turn protected humanity from their deeper meaning for which it was not yet prepared.[2] Today all of that has changed; man is now living in the age of the "consciousness soul" and is able to pursue directly, with clarity of thought, his relation to the spiritual world and to the spiritual beings that share the cosmos with him. Young souls soon after birth are wide-awake and they bring with them a more advanced faculty of thinking. This advanced consciousness will allow them, if they so desire, to follow a spiritual path and to investigate the ever-present world of the spirit. This is expressed by Johann Wolfgang von Goethe:

> How towards the whole all things are blending,
> How heavenly forces are soaring and descending.[3]

How can an aspiring student of spiritual science receive the spiritual knowledge required to find and free his Princess? In other words, how can he or she find the path of inspiration to the Higher Self?

In his painting, *The Good and Evil Angels Struggling for Possession of a Child* (illustration 54), William Blake portrays the struggle for a soul between an Angel Being and the opposing forces that seek its possession. This can be regarded as a truth for what a student on the path will encounter. However, one can rest assured that Angel Beings are there to actively protect the striving soul. As the seeker moves further along the spiritual path, his soul is purified and he becomes more childlike. The Christ spoke about this when He said, "Yes, I say to you, if you do not turn about inwardly and reawaken the pure forces of childhood within yourselves, you will not find access to the kingdom of the heavens."[4]

In the old mysteries the student was completely dependent on his teacher as his sole authority. However, Rudolf Steiner describes how in our age, that of the consciousness soul, a true pupil of the spirit can be a fully independent personality. His actions and beliefs do not rest on the authority of a teacher, but rather on personal insight and rational understanding. A pupil of the twenty-first century demands proof. Today the questions asked by those seeking spiritual knowledge are very direct and relate to spiritual guidance and questions of the self. For this reason

54
The Good and Evil Angels Struggling for Possession of a Child
William Blake
1757–1827

Rudolf Steiner felt that it was important to guide pupils of the spirit in their development, so that they could verify through their own investigations what he was able to bring from his spiritual research. That is why the study of anthroposophy is a necessary first step to a conscious commitment of spiritual development. Rudolf Steiner also drew attention to the existence of true and false paths of investigation into the spiritual world and the dangers that must be avoided or overcome.[5] In two of his major works that provide guidance for the study of Spiritual Science, *The Philosophy of Freedom* and *How to Know Higher Worlds*, he speaks about the development of new organs of cognition through the transformation of thinking, feeling, and willing. This is accomplished by undertaking very specific exercises.[6] The path which Rudolf Steiner has suggested can be walked by every human being, regardless of race or religion. It always begins with study. In *How to Know Higher Worlds*, he says, "Everyone may be certain that an initiate will find him out, under any circumstances, if there is in him an earnest and worthy endeavor to attain this knowledge." He goes on to say, "But there is an equally strict law which insists that no one shall receive any occult knowledge until he is worthy."[7]

Rudolf Steiner did not leave to chance questions that were alive in his soul; he directed them to the spiritual world and in return received clear and concise answers. He was able to consciously pursue the investigation of any subject that was presented to him and to speak about every topic about which questions arose.

While individual students of Spiritual Science receive help with their development through books and through teachers, individual nations receive divine guidance through archangels. "The individual members of a nation are inspired by that archangel to do whatever they do as members of that nation."[8] Wherever there are initiates in the service of mankind, world evolution intensifies. One only need look at the many new directions that were initiated by Rudolf Steiner during his life on earth.

Looking at our time, one may well ask what steps are required for the future development of mankind. This is a complex question to which an answer is found in the next fairy tale. Rudolf Steiner spoke about the transformation of man's astral body leading to the development of the spirit self. This is to take place in the next millennium which he refers to as the Slavic Epoch. At that time East and West are to unite.[9] The Russian fairy tale that follows contains indications of this future epoch.

The Crystal Ball and the Silver Saucer

Once upon a time there was a father. He had three daughters. The first one was proud, the second was greedy, but the youngest daughter was humble, modest, and loving to all around her. One day the father had to go to the city fair. He asked his three daughters, "What can I bring you as a gift?" The eldest daughter said, "Bring me a scarlet dress, Father." Addressing his second daughter he asked, "And what would you like to have?" The second daughter answered, "Father, bring me a necklace of shining stones." "And you my little one, what would you like to have?" the father asked his youngest daughter, while she was clearing away the dishes. She replied, "Oh, Father, you love me and that is all I need." He, however, insisted, "I really would like to bring you something from the fair," and so she answered, "Please bring me a crystal ball on a silver saucer."

The father went to the fair and quickly found a scarlet dress. Likewise he had no trouble finding a necklace made of shining stones. But wherever he looked, he could not find a crystal ball on a silver saucer. He searched from morning to late afternoon until the storekeepers began to pack away their goods and one by one led their horses and carts to go on their way home. Finally the father saw a little old man with a very small stall in a corner at the end of a street.

"Good sir, what can I help you with?" asked the little old man.

"I don't think you can do anything for me," the father said. "I am searching for a crystal ball on a silver saucer, and I have looked everywhere. I don't think it can be bought at the fair."

The old man searched his pocket and said, "I do have a crystal ball and a saucer of silver."

The father nearly danced for joy. "Thank you, thank you, good friend, what do I owe you?"

"You owe me nothing. When the crystal ball is used rightly, that will be reward enough for me." The father began his homeward journey and rode as fast as his horse would carry him.

The two elder daughters were watching from their top windows and as soon as they caught sight of their father, they ran down the stairs and out of the door, welcoming him enthusiastically.

"Have you brought my scarlet dress, Father?"

"Here is your scarlet dress, my daughter."

"Have you got my necklace of shining stones?"

"I have indeed your shining beads, my child."

After a while his youngest daughter appeared: "Father, you must be in need of a rest, have you had any food? I will get your slippers and there is a meal cooked on the table. Come and refresh yourself."

The father took his dear girl into his arms and said, "Here is your crystal ball on a silver saucer." She put his gift away into her pocket and busied herself until she saw that her father was rested and refreshed and all the dishes were cleared away. Then she crept into a corner all by herself and took the ball out of her pocket.

Her two elder sisters said to each other, "What is our youngest sister doing? Have you ever heard of a present as foolish as a crystal ball? Let us go and find her." Without her knowledge they crept up behind her.

The youngest sister took the ball, laid it on the silver saucer, and spoke the words, "Roll, roll little ball in my saucer of silver and show me the cities of the world." The ball began to roll and a beautiful light attached itself to it. As the sisters watched, it increased in strength until it was a shimmering crystal in which appeared the cities of the world. Towering above in shining sunlight was the golden palace of the Czar. The picture glowed, grew really bright and clear and then began to fade.

She said once more, "Roll, roll little ball in my saucer of silver and show me the oceans and seas." Again the ball began to roll and shining pictures appeared. The sisters could see the waves of the ocean and the wide waters bearing countless fleets of ships. The picture grew ever clearer until it began to fade.

One more time the youngest sister spoke, "Roll little ball on my saucer of silver and show me the heavens with the sun, the moon and the stars in all their glory." Then the ball began to roll a third time and from amid the shining crystal they saw the fires of the heavens, the Moon, the Sun and the stars in all their splendor and glory.

The older sisters were seized with longing to possess this beautiful treasure, and the oldest said, "Will you trade the crystal ball for my scarlet dress?" "Will you give me the crystal ball if I give you my necklace of shining stones?" asked the second.

"How can I do that?" said the youngest. "It was a gift from my father to me. I cannot give it away."

The two sisters were very jealous and angry and they decided that whatever happened, they would find a way of acquiring the crystal ball on its silver saucer.

On a beautiful summer's day when flowers were blooming everywhere and the birds filled the air with their song and the forest was full of new growth, the two wicked sisters said to the youngest: "It is a lovely day; we are going out to pick strawberries. Will you come with us?" The youngest sister agreed and went with them deep into the forest. They walked and walked but to no avail; there were no strawberries to be found.

"It is time to return. Our father will be waiting for his evening meal," said the youngest.

"Don't worry. It will be light for a long time yet!" exclaimed the older sister.

"We need to go home. Our father will be concerned not knowing where we are!"

"Look, Sister! Here in the grass you will find some strawberries. Gather them and then we shall return home."

They had come to a woodland glade where there were some trees next to a patch with beautiful long grass. Leaning against a tree stood a spade that had been left by someone who had been digging for water. The youngest girl bent down to look for the fruit when the two elder sisters came from behind and struck her with the spade. They killed her and buried her under the grass. Then they went home to their father. They told him that their sister had foolishly wandered off into the forest and that the wolves must have seized her.

The father searched for many a day for his youngest daughter. He grieved and mourned for his lost daughter for a long time.

The wicked sisters searched for the crystal ball on the silver saucer. When they found it where it had been left, they spoke the verse which they had heard their sister recite so often, "Roll, roll little ball, on the saucer of silver and show me the cities of the world." The ball was silent and it did not move; neither a light nor a picture appeared. They tried it again and again, but nothing happened and finally they gave up, feeling both confused and angry.

Winter passed and spring returned. A shepherd boy was wandering through the woodland, trying to find bulrushes. He wanted to make a pipe. After a lengthy search he came to a glade where the grass was long and green, and there were red, blue, and white flowers. The wind murmured in the rushes. He found what he was looking for, cut one of the stems, and began to shape it into a flute. When he tried to play it, he noticed that, as if by magic, the flute followed its own tune. He listened and a sad and strange song sounded forth with the mysterious words:

> O sing unto the world my song,
> The woeful song of how I died.
> My sisters did me grievous wrong
> And laid me in the cold wood side.

The shepherd boy wandered home as if in a trance and continued to listen as the flute played its own tune. As he passed by the village houses, the flute continued its song:

> And where the flowers are white and red
> I lie and wait below the clay
> For one to wake me from the dead
> And lead me to the light of day.

Suddenly a door opened and the father came rushing out of his house. "That is the voice of my daughter, my lost child! Shepherd boy, where did you learn that song?"

The shepherd boy led him into the forest to the wood glade where the white, red, and blue flowers were blossoming and where the wind rustled in the bulrushes. The spade was still there and with it they turned the grass aside, where the young maiden was lying as if in a deep slumber. She was dazzlingly beautiful, and the father, on seeing his favorite child, began to weep.

The shepherd boy cried, "Do not mourn for the death of your child. In the palace of the Czar flows the fountain of the Water of Life. I will go to the Czar and ask him for three holy drops to rouse her from the dead."

The shepherd boy went to the palace of the Czar, but the servants would not let him in. He was, after all, only a lowly shepherd boy. However, he put the flute to his lips and the song sang once more the story of the maid and how she died.

"What a wonderful tune! Who is singing this strange sweet song?" the Czar asked his servants.

"Oh, it is just a simple shepherd boy," he was told.

But he asked to have him brought up. The shepherd boy fell on his knees before the Czar and told him the story of the dead maiden. Then he asked him for three drops of the Water of Life. The Czar went before the fountain and bade the spirit of the well pour forth her waters:

> Water of Life, O fountainhead,
> Weep thy tears for a maiden dead.
> Water of life, O quickening stream,
> Rouse a maid from her winter dream.

The spirit of the well caused the water to spring forth for him, and so the shepherd boy could take the three drops needed to awaken the maiden from her death-like sleep. The Czar followed the shepherd boy and with the three drops he touched the maiden's head, her heart and her hands— and she stood before them in all her radiance.

When the time came the Czar heard about the crystal ball and the silver saucer and asked his daughter if he could see them. After he had beheld the cities of the world with their towers, the oceans and seas with their fleets of ships, and the Sun, the Moon and the stars in their glory, he cried, "Oh, you beautiful maiden, you alone are worthy to be my bride. Your cruel sisters shall be led to their death, and you and your father shall come to my palace and live with me in joy."

The beautiful maiden begged for the life of her sisters saying that they had suffered enough, because the crystal ball had never revealed its secrets to them.

Then the Czar spoke to the shepherd boy and offered rich rewards, but the shepherd boy replied, "Your Majesty, I am poor and I would rather wander through the streets and play my sweet songs than live in the palaces of kings. But every year in the spring I will pass below your turrets and greet you with my loveliest song of joy."

The shepherd boy was granted his wish, and the wedding of the Czar and his bride was celebrated with much happiness.

In the two fairy tales of *The Firebird* and *The Fisher-Prince*, the main characters underwent personal spiritual development. The story of *The Crystal Ball and the Silver Saucer* takes a different approach. It points to the possible union between Eastern Slavic and Western cultures. This story could be regarded as heralding a new combined culture for which the seeds have been prepared for a long time. This preparation was undertaken by the angelic realm for the benefit of humanity's progress. The youngest daughter may well represent the soul configuration of the Russian people.

The Shepherd Boy as the Representative of an Awakened Will

Through the will, inspiration for right actions is brought about. In this fairy tale, awakening to a new life occurs when the youngest daughter is healed by the Water of Life. This water of life flows from the spring in the Russian Czar's castle. A young shepherd boy makes a flute from bulrushes. Fashioning a musical instrument out of bulrushes is not easy. As he walks through the village, it is the flute's magical song that is heard by the father, who has been told of his young daughter's death by the two older sisters. He meets the shepherd boy and together they return to the meadow to find her. It is also the shepherd boy who knows about the castle of the Czar and goes to request three drops of the Water of Life. With these three drops of water the Czar revives the youngest daughter. The shepherd boy's flute, as in Mozart's *The Magic Flute*, is a symbol of the activity of the will. The fact that he is young is a metaphor for his purity of soul.

The importance of the Czar's palace is first introduced through the magic of the crystal ball, in which the youngest daughter sees it towering high above all the other cities of the world. One might well ask, why does a 'castle' tower above all the cities of the world, and what lives as an imagination in the personality of the Czar?

This vision is followed by a second and a third; the youngest daughter beholds all the oceans of the world and finally the reader's attention is drawn to the Heavens, the Sun, the Moon and the Stars. In her crystal ball visions she sees both near and far; she sees the Czar's castle as well as the distant movements of the cosmos.

Clairvoyance through Heart Forces: the Youngest Daughter

While the shepherd boy is guided by the flute that he carved, the youngest daughter has visions that are not obtained through developed will forces, but rather through intuition, the feeling capacities of her pure soul. She was the only one of the three sisters who always cared for and looked after the well-being of her father. Her caring for another before all else, her joy in the simple crystal ball, and the trust in her older sisters, even when it led her to her death, represent her purity of soul. Killed by her older sisters, she is buried until her revival. When she receives the three drops of water from the Czar, she awakens to her higher self.

Her character traits belong to the Russian cultural spirit. She stands in contrast to her older sisters who are materialistic and selfish. As for the gifts from their father, one sister asked for a scarlet dress, the other for precious stones. They take the gifts, but not being satisfied with them, they trick and kill their younger sister to gain her crystal ball and silver platter. Yet their undeveloped and impure souls are not prepared to receive that gift, and hence the lack of response from the crystal ball.

The Water of Life

Water is the central focus of one of the youngest daughter's visions. Countless fleets of ships move over the ocean waves. Her vision is connected to movement and life in relation to water. It is not static, but becomes a living experience for her. It is well-known that creation occurs through water and that life reveals itself through the substance of water. This is referred to in The First Book of Moses, Genesis.[10] The living quality of water is shown in illustration 55. In a meandering stream, winding its way between the separate vortices, one encounters the flowing, moving and creative qualities of water. These rhythmic, living, formative streams in water are a physical representation of a life energy or etheric force.

In illustration 56 the creative life force resembles a meandering stream winding its way between the various knots of a tree trunk. Although the activity of the life forces is more easily seen in the liquid element, it penetrates everything in nature and its imprint is also left on solid matter. Such a remnant of swirling vortices can be observed in the bark and knots. In illustration 57 one sees also the impressive dynamic force of water and its display on a snail shell.[11] The ancient Greeks often clothed sculptures of human figures with an "etheric sheath" that resembles flowing water. This arose out of a direct experience of the life force connected to the physical body. Another beautiful depiction of life forces can be found in the twelfth-century French Basilica of Madeleine, in the relief of The Christ (illustration 58, page 124). Observe the swirls around the knee and on the right hip-joint of the Christ. This dynamic formative force exists also in the non-physical, for example in the ability to think creatively and with flexibility.

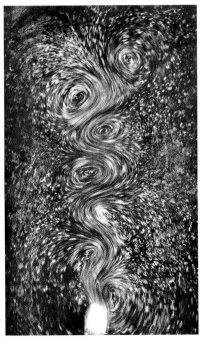

55

56

Sensitive Chaos:
The Creation of Flowing Forms
in Water and Air
Theodor Schwenk

57a

57b

58
The Christ
12th c.

The youngest daughter experiences not only water, through her vision of the waves on the ocean, but also a higher vision of creative formative forces. Perhaps one may assume that she is experiencing the forces of the Universe as they work in the act of creation.[12]

Johann Wolfgang von Goethe, the German poet, compared the soul of man to water:

> The soul of man is like water:
> It comes from heaven,
> It returns to heaven,
> And again down to earth it must go,
> Forever changing.[13]

The knowledge of the world that the youngest daughter seeks and receives through her visions embraces the past as well as the future. This is the reason why the crystal ball rests on a silver platter. Silver is the element connected to the moon forces and the past. The Water of Life, on the other hand, points ahead to the future task of Russia.[14]

The concept of living water is taken a step further in the story. This takes place when the Czar awakens the youngest daughter with three drops of the Water of Life, which he places on her head, heart, and hands. Again the question arises, who/what does the Czar represent? This rejuvenation signifies a transformation of thinking, feeling, and willing. The head facilitates thinking, the heart relates to feeling, and the hands enable the act of doing. All three become imbued with the Christ forces sounding in the words, "I am the Resurrection and the Life."[15]

This could be seen as an advanced initiation process. Following these thoughts a step further, one may say that the water that is connected to Christ is much more than a heightened awareness of thinking, feeling and willing; it means to achieve a higher level of one's development in cosmic evolution. It means also to comprehend cosmic wisdom and in the far future to become a co-creator of the world, a true brother of Christ, who bestows boundless love and eternity—indeed everlasting life.[16]

59
The Threefold Man
Rudolf Steiner
(1861–1925)

Rudolf Steiner's Artistic Rendering of the Threefold Human Being

The threefold nature of the human being is creatively expressed in Rudolf Steiner's drawing, *The Threefold Man* (illustration 59).

It is interesting that the colors of the flowers in this fairy tale, described on the grave, are white, blue, and red. In his optical experiments with light, Newton came to the conclusion that when all the colors of the rainbow are combined, the color white is formed. For Goethe white is the representation of light itself.[17] Rudolf Steiner also explains that light, so important to man, presents itself to our world as the color white. He goes on to say that light leads man to his spirit and that in the light, consciousness arises. White or light is the soul picture of the spirit.[18]

Yellow, on the other hand, lives as happiness in the soul. It wants to radiate outward, diffusing to ever lighter shades, to almost white. Rudolf Steiner stated, "Yellow is the radiance of the spirit."[19] This is why halos in the Middle Ages were yellow in color or painted with gold. It can also be said that white and yellow are the colors related to an active thinking process. One talks about light-filled thinking.

The color blue has a different quality; it has a tendency to expand in a quieter, more dreamlike fashion. When one looks at the blue of the sky, one is drawn up into an infinite expanse. This expanse, Rudolf Steiner said, causes us to experience humility. Blue also speaks to our feelings. When the color blue, as in illustration 59, is explored, it seems to strive towards the center, becoming ever lighter, whilst it remains strongest on the outside.[20] Renaissance painters often depicted the Madonna draped in a blue cloak, emphasizing her humility, universality, connection to the heavens, and strong feeling.

The color red, according to Corinne Heline in her book *Color and Music in the New Age*, represents strength and endurance. Red is the color of the will. It carries a surging vitality and can be imagined as the color of the creator spirit.

In his drawing, Rudolf Steiner uses the colors white, yellow, blue, and red to describe creatively the threefold man, a being that expresses itself through thinking, feeling, and willing. Did the flowers on the grave of the youngest daughter represent a similar idea? Perhaps the creator of this fairy tale chose the colors with clear intention. After all, the daughter is a threefold human being who lies buried under the clay. She can be awakened only with three drops of water from the Water of Life. Goodness, as represented by the youngest daughter, does not die, but can lie dormant awaiting its call to life.

While the Russian soul lives in the youngest daughter, the sisters represent a more individualized, self-centered, and materialistic stream alive in the West. During the future Slavic epoch the West will seek out the socially more conscious Russian soul. It will require the heart forces found in the Christ impulse that are so prevalent in the Slavic soul, while it will share its developed intellectual soul and new spirituality with Russia. This is still being prepared by the hierarchy for the East and West, in order for humanity to advance to the next stage of its evolution.

60
Processional Path with Sphinxes at the Temple at Luxor, Egypt, 400 BC

The Incarnation of the Ego

Human evolution requires time. When one looks back at the long path of history, footsteps of developmental achievements clearly stand out. It may appear as if the ego has always been a conscious part of the human being, yet man in the past was not as firmly connected to his physical body and as conscious of his own goals as he is today. He had to learn to say "I" when he was referring to himself alone. The stages of mankind's past development parallel those in the development of the young child. When a child is about three years old, he or she reaches that moment of discovery, for example, when she no longer says, "Anna thinks" or "me say," but rather says, "I think" and "I say." Thousands of years of evolution have brought man to where he is. Today he is able to identify himself with his ego and stand firmly in the world.

The footsteps of this development can still be traced when one looks back to ancient Egypt, to about 3000 BC. The pharaohs of that ancient cultural epoch were inspired by the hierarchies to guide the human ego into incarnation. The earliest Egyptians lived collectively as a group with a single ego that was carried by the leader. No festivals, decisions regarding harvest, or other community activities were made without the guidance of the pharaoh.

Inspired by divine beings, the pharaohs at Luxor and Karnak brought together their people for large festive temple processions (illustration 60). Guided by temple priests, their souls stirred by incense and song, the procession moved down a long wide avenue lined with sphinxes that had ram heads and lion bodies.[21] The powerful atmosphere created by these sculptures must have stirred their souls profoundly. In the distance they saw the pylon, or temple façade, with two high obelisks near its entrance. Lifting their gaze upward to the peaks of the obelisks—the pyramidions,[22] they perceived the sun's rays streaming down from their Sun God, Amun-Ra. In this way the Egyptians experienced height, after having walked alongside many sphinxes stretched in a horizontal position. They inwardly felt as though they had been lifted upwards from the earth to the sun. This was followed by another soul-rending experience. At the entrance of the temple they stood face-to-face with majestic sculptures of god-like pharaohs, seated in front of the pylon. Standing before these massive figures, the Egyptian went through a range of emotions. He was in awe, inspired, perhaps even frightened and humbled. The experience of this broad range of feeling life gave him the beginnings of a sense of self.

Gottfried Richter described the temple walk of ancient Egypt very clearly in his book, *Art and Human Consciousness*. He wrote,

> At the end of this avenue rose an enormous wall, the pylon of the temple. The eye had seen it already from a distance. To those who were moving towards it, it seemed to rise higher and higher, threatening, gigantic, overpoweringly superhuman. In its center is a portal, narrow, steep, and inexorably stern. Gigantic stone figures stand on either side of it. But man must pass through it. The whole massive front of the temple is there for this one compelling gate.[23]

After the procession, the Egyptian had to separate from the group and enter all alone through this narrow entrance into the temple. This spot was as far as a normal human being was able to go. It took all the strength available for someone who still lived in the group soul experience to complete this distance. The sacred walk imprinted itself deeply not only on his soul, but also on his physical body. The temple priests alone had the strength to penetrate further into the main hall of the sanctuary.

This cultural custom was a guided ego incarnation process. Gottfried Richter wrote, "The Egyptian experiences how man enters his own house (his own body)—how, coming from the outside, he is guided to its threshold. In those days the souls of men were still intensely absorbed in the outside world and expanses of the heavens. These temples must have been a tremendous education toward self-awareness, guiding man into new and almost unbearable inner movements and experiences. The closer a man came to it, the more this wall pushed its way into him. Its gesture forced him deeper and deeper into his own physical body."[24] This was the help that was given to mankind by a guiding archangel in order that the individual could separate from the group soul, slowly incarnate into his own physical body, and become conscious of it.

When Rudolf Steiner investigated the past, present, and future developmental stages set for mankind, he was able to relate those to specific periods of time. The Egyptian epoch lasted from 2907 to 747 BC. When he spoke about a Russian or Slavic soul epoch, he pointed to a period from AD 3573 to 5733. At that time, he indicated that healing forces would flow from the Russian soul to the Western world. In the fairy tale, the Water of Life is a metaphor for the healing force.

The People of the Christ

What is Russia's future task? Understanding the Russian character and soul leads one closer to understanding this question. In his book *From Symptom to Reality in Modern History,* Rudolf Steiner stated, "The Russian soul bears within it the seed of the future."[25] He then goes on to say: "The Russian people, in the widest sense of the term, became, within the framework of European civilization, the people of the Christ. We express a profound truth when we say that in this epoch and in readiness for later times, a people had been especially prepared by world events to become the people of the Christ."[26] I have travelled extensively throughout Russia and my experiences support Rudolf Steiner's indications.

I was sitting in a lecture hall in a town in Eastern Russia listening to a German physician, sharing with his audience a new approach to medical problems, as well as a different way of looking at the human being.[27] He developed his thesis very logically and methodically. After about twenty-five minutes, one of the Russian listeners stood up and asked a single question, "Please tell me, what does all this have to do with the Christ?" The speaker had not expected this.

Here was a perfect example of the difference between a central European and a Russian approach to the thinking process. The physician spoke from an intellectual perspective while the Russian was listening with his heart. In social settings a Russian is more comfortable responding out of his or her intuition. Rudolf Steiner explained this when he said, "The Christ is ever present as an inner aura impregnating the thinking and feeling of these people."[28] This helps one understand that in general Russians do not like to penetrate life's questions with intellectual debates. Intellectual debates are very different from inspired thought processes.

Intuition is connected more to the heart than to the brain. When someone inquires about the weather, a probable answer would be, "It is 20 degrees Celsius with 4 centimeters of precipitation expected in the afternoon." This may be a true and a typical answer that one would expect today. Another response might be: "It's warm and it will be raining cats and dogs this afternoon."

In the same way that a Russian might answer more intuitively, he might also avoid being subjected to too many rules and regulations in his social life. Rudolf Steiner explained that the Russian simply does not want to understand nor relate to such a way of life. He lives intuitively and allows ego impulses to arise in the moment. Indeed, they often arise from the heart. [29]

Anyone who travels within Russia can experience this heart-warm-imbued life. It lives in wonderfully rich music, in literature, in art, and also in the interactions among people. For example, on one occasion, people whom we had never met before found us stranded and invited all five of us to stay with them in their apartment for a week.

Russian friends of ours choose not to wear seatbelts when driving, even though a member of their family died in a car accident. Many drivers in Russia have icons on their dashboards or hanging from their mirrors. One taxi driver went so far as to have an icon covering his speedometer! People trust that they are protected. Even a Russian coin is imprinted with the image of the Archangel Michael fighting the dragon!

These examples attempt to show that the Russian lives much more in his soul nature and in the trust that he is being protected than does a middle European. The soul gesture of a middle European is fundamentally different. Rules and regulations permeate his culture, and most individuals live by these rules.

The Russian soul was not exposed to Christianity until the eleventh century. By then the Western Church had held several ecumenical councils, during which decisions about church regulations were made. The first took place in AD 325, in Nicaea, present-day Turkey. After much deliberation, it was decided what the faithful should believe and how they should conduct themselves in relation to church matters and festivals.[30]

The Russian, in comparison, lived in an innocent, individual, relationship to the Christ. People were connected predominantly to *starets*, Russian hermits, and to other holy people. Since its introduction to Russia, Christians have experienced much suffering through suppressive political systems, but have survived and resurfaced in modern Russia.

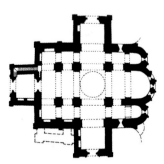

61
Cathedral of the Birth of Mary, Russia, and

62
the floor plan
ca. AD 1225

Russian and Middle European Churches

The nature of the Russian soul is cosmopolitan. It is inclusive and embracing. This characteristic of the Russian people lives so strongly that it found expression in the architecture of the Eastern Orthodox churches, so numerous in Russia (illustration 61).

The tendency to unite the community is clearly expressed through the intentional floor plan (illustration 62). The floor area is arranged in the shape of a cross with equal vertical and horizontal spaces. The faithful gather together in the center, a nave under a dome in which Christ, the World Ruler, is represented. The iconostasis, upon which icons are hung, separates the altar and the priest from the nave (illustration 63). There are no pews. Along the back wall or in a corner, a bench can be found for the sick, tired, and elderly. The walls and columns throughout the church are decorated with beautiful icons from floor to ceiling. In these churches one feels connected not only with the other worshippers, but also with the Holy Family and the world of angels and saints. All become close friends on the earthly journey.

63
Typical interior of an Eastern Orthodox church

64
Cathedral and Cathedral Court
Ratzeburg, Germany
8th c.

The Western faithful, in comparison, follow a more individual path. Laws and regulations developed during the ecumenical councils do not encourage a Western soul to live in the same social freedom as the Russian. This path of individual development nurtures independence, strength, and self-confidence. On the other hand, it can grow into alienation and loneliness of soul.

These characteristics of independence and strength are emphasized in the architecture of the early Western Christian church. Although its interior space is also in the form of a cross, it differs from the Eastern Orthodox design by an extended approach to the altar lined with rows of pews. The floor plan resembles the cross on which Christ was crucified. All the worshippers walk "alone" down the aisle towards the front of the church, accompanied only by their thoughts. Here they are met by the priest who is their link to God (illustrations 64 and 65).

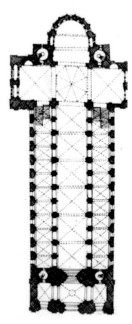

65
Speyer Cathedral floor plan
ca. 1040

66
Rout of the Rebel Angels
William Blake (1757–1827)

The Heart- and the Head-Forces Will Unite in the Future

On the long path of evolution, the human being is not alone. He has not yet gained the strength of ego to ward off adversary forces that try to hinder his development. He is continually confronted by obstacles and temptations that are placed in his way by fallen spiritual beings. Fortunately, if he so desires, he can always seek and count on the help of the angelic world. William Blake (illustration 66) portrays beings who were cast down to the earth realm and now tempt man.[31]

In the story of *The Crystal Ball and the Silver Saucer,* the older sisters fall prey to such temptations and are persuaded to kill their younger sibling in order to gain possession of the crystal ball and the silver saucer. They did not know or understand that in order for the crystal ball to roll on the silver saucer, as it had for their younger sister, a pure soul was required. Their younger sister could look into the future with true clairvoyance, as well as gain knowledge of the past. But the evil influence acting through the older sisters prevented them from being able to command the ball to roll. This also explains what the seller meant when he refused payment from the father and said: "You owe me nothing. When the crystal ball is used rightly, that will be reward enough for me."

If one considers the development of a more social life, as in Russia, or a more individualized life as, for example in Europe and North America, one discovers that Western man had to develop the skills with which to function successfully in an increasingly complex world. However, at the same time, Western man became enmeshed ever more deeply in materialism which has brought with it alienation, estrangement and loneliness.

In time, out of the West will arise a new spirituality which will unite with the Russian soul, whose mission it is to develop humanity's heart forces. The West will be drawn to the East and, like the youngest daughter in the story, transform its thinking, feeling and willing faculties through the Water of Life—the Christ impulse. The West will share with the East its ability to think clearly and decisively in all earthly matters, while at the same time it will receive from the East a new impulse towards an all-embracing unity.

East and West are destined to continue together into the distant future.[32] In order for this to happen, it is important that human beings in both East and West become conscious of their separate streams and spiritual tasks. Mankind will succeed in its mission of uniting the East with the West only if opposing and hindering forces are overcome.

67
Ancient coat of arms of
Novgorod, Russia

68
Man with Light
1962
Alexander Kharitinov

Works of Art Express the Future

The ancient coat of arms of the city of Novgorod, Russia, shows an empty throne protected by two bears. Three candles are attached to the top of the throne, and two fish facing each other are below (illustration 67). Today, the throne which is symbolic for the coming Russian epoch is in fact still empty. The fish, the zodiacal Pisces, is connected to the feet of the human being. Representing East and West, the fish point to a future time when those who follow the Christ will walk toward each other directly with love. Having overcome the lower forces or animal within, they will take up the sword and create a world-embracing community. The symbol of the empty throne embraces the present but points to the future.

The true mission of the Russian soul will not take place until the middle of the next millennium, since it requires a long period of preparation by the hierarchies. Meanwhile Russia awaits its task. The empty throne is a symbol for this waiting.

The fairy tale of *The Crystal Ball and the Silver Saucer* also conveys the idea of this waiting but through a different imagination. The youngest daughter who represents the Slavic epoch waits under the earth. The shepherd boy finds her through the song that arises out of his bulrush flute, which represents the will. He brings the Czar and the Water of Life to her to make her whole. For the time being, in reality, the youngest daughter is still under the earth and the throne is awaiting its time.

Through the above examples, one gains a clearer understanding of how two imaginations, that of the fairy tale and that of the ancient coat of arms of the city of Novgorod, express the same truth.

As is pointed out in illustration 54, the battle for the soul is of interest to both good and evil forces. It will be essential to save the spiritual essence of humanity through individual striving towards the higher self.

The coming Russian epoch and its current state of "waiting" are also imaginatively portrayed in the painting *Man with Light* (illustration 68) by Alexander Kharitinov. In the upper right, two forms resemble a pair of lungs. Although painted in red and gold, the two parts are surrounded and veiled by a cloud-like shadow. If they are meant to be lungs, breathing certainly does not come easily. The man climbing the mountain is carrying a dim light. He finds his way carefully and moves upwards slowly. Below the mountain, on the hillside, there appears a depression in which are two doves. One dove on the left looks towards the house, while the other points its head in the opposite direction. Both are keenly interested in what is going on around them. They are alert, and, in relation to the man with the light, they appear to show more presence. For centuries, The Holy Spirit has been portrayed as a dove. Could these two beautiful birds be representing the watchful eye of the hierarchies who are very much aware of what is happening on the earth? Do the two lungs above the earth portray concern for the earth? Two flowers were painted by the artist. One is still unopened, while the other shines brightly just below the house. A warm light can be seen shining through the window of the house, and its breathing, indicated by the smoke, rises from the chimney straight up to the sky or perhaps to heaven. All is well and at peace in this painting. It is steeped in a warm glow and can become a source of great comfort to those who read its message.

Michael is the archangel of the Russian people. He is represented on earth by St. George who is portrayed as the courageous one who conquers the dragon. Together they are carrying Russia into a new epoch, an epoch which will lead mankind ever closer to its ultimate goal of transforming the earth into a planet of love and freedom.

A true fairy tale, grasped with an understanding developed through Spiritual Science, can become a fount of revelations and lead to the discovery of unsuspected secrets. The fairy tale of *The Crystal Ball and the Silver Saucer* goes beyond a personal path of development. It portrays the guidance of the divine through the activities of the hierarchies in leading humanity. These higher beings, along with many others, have been quietly helping mankind and will continue to inspire and guide people of every nationality.

Representative of Man
Rudolf Sreiner

6 Bashtchelik or True Steel

A bridge is crossed when reading fairy tales, such as *The Fisher-Prince*, with the expanded consciousness given to us by Spiritual Science. This bridge takes us out of fairyland into a psychological reality. Every word becomes meaningful when the content of the fairy tale leaves the subconscious realm of feeling and awakens to a real human experience which can be grasped by the intellect.

There are as many fairy tales as individual human beings on this earth. Each person owns his or her soul story, and all belong to a cosmic whole. The content of each life story depends on past incarnations and forces that are brought into this life from the depth of the human soul. The past includes not only previous incarnations but also life between death and rebirth; the human being, a microcosm, extends into the macrocosm where truth alone speaks.

The story of *Bashtchelik or True Steel*[1] carries as its main theme the different faces of evil and the possibilities given to a human being to overcome and transform them. A light will be shone on Bashtchelik revealing an underlying hidden and mysterious human soul-life which every reader may yearn to experience consciously. Collectively, the characters in the story portray the complexity of the human soul.

Bashtchelik or True Steel

Once upon a time there was an old Czar who called for his three sons and three daughters because he was near death and wanted to leave his last earthly bequests with them.

"My dear sons," he said, "to you I leave my kingdom and I ask you that you love one another and rule in fairness and justice. There is one last command I will make before I leave you. Whoever may come to seek your sisters in marriage, grant your permission freely. If you do not act as I say, a terrible punishment will fall upon you because you have not obeyed my last wish." The Czar had ruled for many years and when he closed his eyes and his soul departed, the brothers and sisters sitting by his bedside felt lonely and sad.

Suddenly they were disturbed by a great storm, which swept through the whole valley. The walls shook, the doors rattled, and the wind howled, while the castle was in the dark. The brothers and sisters clung together in fear while they anxiously waited for the lightning and listened to the thunder.

After a bright flash and a mighty roll of thunder, they heard a deep voice calling out to them: "In the name of the King, open the gates! I have come to claim the eldest sister in marriage."

The eldest son shouted, "That is impossible!" and the second exclaimed, "Whoever wants one's sister to be married to a thunderstorm?" Only the youngest son was calm and said, "Remember the wish of our dying father. What have we to fear? I will open the gates!"

The Prince took the eldest sister by the hand and led her out through the palace courtyard to the gates. They looked out into the dismal night. The storm was fierce as they tried to see who was there. It appeared that there was no one. Suddenly a flash of lightning lit up the darkness of the sky and the princess was lifted off the ground right from his side and disappeared into the clouds. At the same time there was a very loud clap of thunder and the castle gates clashed together, locking firmly.

Meanwhile the courtiers were so afraid that they fell on their knees. They did not dare to look around them, and they only prayed that they might be spared the wrath of heaven. The Prince came back to the castle alone.

The second night the brothers and sisters were again assembled in the big hall keeping watch, when suddenly a gust of wind swept right across the room. The curtains billowed into the night and the storm developed into the most violent tempest. While sweeping around the castle, it took a chimney in its path. It was as if the gusts of wind came from all the corners of the earth when they heard a strong voice saying: "In the name of the King, open the castle gate. I have come to claim your second sister in marriage."

"That is impossible," said the oldest son. "Whoever heard of a King's daughter marrying a whirlwind? Remember what happened last night!" "Impossible!" cried the second son, too. The youngest Prince alone remained calm and spoke: "Have you forgotten our father's last command? Although the heavens threaten us, I will obey him and open the gates."

He took the second sister by the hand and led her across the courtyard. Then he opened the massive gates. He attempted to see who was there, but there was no one to be seen. The clouds whirled around the sky, being moved and torn into pieces by blowing winds, creating ever-new forms in the process. All of a sudden a passing gust swept the princess from his side, and he realized that she was gone into the dark of the night. The courtiers stared at the window in fear, while the Prince, deeply saddened and alone, returned to the castle to his brothers and their one remaining youngest sister.

The third night was more terrible than the others. Although there was stillness in the air, the earth began to rumble and before long the ground trembled under their feet. Every tower and turret of the castle seemed to rock. The brothers and their sister hardly dared to move for fear that the palace might crash in on their heads when they heard a mighty voice coming from the deep: "I have come to claim the hand of your youngest sister in marriage."

"We have already lost two sisters," said the eldest brother. "I refuse to let our youngest and dearest sister go!" "You are right," the second brother agreed. "How can we give our youngest and most beloved sister to an earthquake in marriage? It would be a crime!"

The youngest Prince was unperturbed and said, "Do you value so little the promise we gave to our father? Terrible punishment will befall those who disobey the wishes of the dying. It is not for fear of punishment but because I loved our father that I wish to carry out his last wish. I will open the gates and give my sister to this strange suitor." The Prince took his youngest sister by the hand and led her out into the night. He opened the gates of the castle, but again there was no one to be seen; it was pitch dark.

Suddenly the earth trembled and everything around him seemed to sway. When he turned to his sister to protect her, he noticed that she had disappeared from his side into the night. He stood alone by the castle gates. When he returned, he found the courtiers and his brothers with their faces on the ground, for they thought that the end of the world had come. The two eldest brothers mourned for their sisters, saying that they would never see them again and that they were gone forever. The youngest brother alone was sure that they had done the right thing and he tried to console them. "Dear brothers," he said, "have we not done what our father asked us to do before he died, his last wish? Don't you think that we would be blessed on that account alone? How can our sisters be gone? They are bound to be somewhere in the world. Let us go forth and seek them."

The brothers felt their courage returning, and all three set out into the world to seek their sisters. They went through valleys, over mountains, through meadows with beautiful flowers, and through deserts where all human habitation was left behind. After crossing the desert, they came to a great forest. The branches were hanging low; as they travelled on, there was no sign of life anywhere. Finally, one evening they reached a lakeside. It was a large lake and the area seemed wild and unfriendly. The eldest brother said, "One of us needs to keep watch. There might be robbers or wild beasts in quest of prey; I am the oldest and will look after you tonight."

The others, wrapped in their cloaks, lay down and soon fell asleep while the eldest brother kept watch. He listened as keenly as he could to make sure that no enemy was at hand. Far away he heard a fox bark, and a little later he heard the hooting of an owl. Then there was silence, a deep silence. It seemed there was not a sound in the whole wide world.

As the eldest brother gazed out onto the lake, he noticed how the waters began to stir—first one ripple, then another, and then the head of a monster rose out of the water and kept moving towards him. It came ever closer, ready to devour him. He was a brave warrior, so he pulled out his sword and attacked the terrible creature. Down it came with its great gaping wide mouth and gleaming eyes; the monster was struck. Flash! Again the prince's sword came down like lightning and the black head fell to the ground severed from its body. The great headless creature sank back into the waters of the lake, while the prince sprang forward, took hold of the head, and cut off its two large ears. He placed these carefully into his pouch and pushed the head back into the water.

The grey dawn was beginning to shine over the hills when he woke his two brothers. "Have you had a quiet watch?" they asked him. "Very quiet," answered the eldest prince, and he said not a word of his strange adventure.

All the next day they journeyed on again through wild and gloomy forests until nightfall when they reached another lake. "Let us rest here," said the second brother, "and tonight it is my turn to keep guard."

The two brothers were tired, lay down on the ground, wrapped themselves in their mantles, and soon fell asleep. The second brother sat by the lake and listened intently. He expected to hear the howl of wolves or the sound of a lion prowling in search of prey, but he could hear only the water running up the shore and a gentle wind in the leaves of the trees. Slowly the evening breeze died away and the waves and the rushes seemed to have fallen asleep.

Looking out over the lake he saw how the water began to tremble, and to his astonishment he saw two big heads of a terrible monster approaching him. It came closer every moment, ready to devour him. The prince leapt to the side and drew his sword. Flash! The prince struck the monster, and again, flash! the second head was also severed from the body of the monster. Slowly the headless body fell back into the lake while the prince jumped forward and cut the four ears off the two heads, then rolled them back into the lake.

When his two brothers woke up and asked him, "Did you have a quiet watch?" he replied, "Not a sound to be heard!" He had decided not to talk about his adventure during the night.

And so they travelled all day going through vast gloomy forests until by nightfall they came to a third lake. "Tonight it is my turn to watch," said the youngest Prince.

In this lake lived a far more terrible monster—it had three heads—and when the other two brothers were sound asleep, the Prince saw it coming out of the lake. It approached him with great speed. The monster looked as if it were ready to devour all three brothers together in one gulp, but the youngest Prince had no fear. He drew his sword and—flash! to the right, flash! to the left, flash! upward and downward—he severed the three heads from the monstrous body. The lake sucked back the giant form while the Prince rushed forward to cut off the six ears, which he carefully placed in his pouch. He flung the heads into the lake and turned to greet his brothers. It was still dark and both of them were fast asleep, so he decided to find some kindling wood to make a fire. He was cold and began to wander here and there, gathering a few dry twigs, when far in the distance he saw a gleam of light.

"That is surely a shepherds' fire," he thought. "I will go and beg some glowing ember from them." He made his way over rocks and stones until he found himself standing outside a cave. The Prince nearly cried aloud in astonishment, for there inside, seated in a circle and feasting on human bones, sat nine great giants.

The Prince knew that whatever happened, he must show no fear, so he boldly stepped into their midst and cried out, "Good morning, brothers! You are the very people whom I have been seeking." The giants were caught by surprise; he spoke so confidently and boldly that they felt he was a friend.

"Good morning, little one," said their leader. "We do not know you, but you seem to be one of our kind. Come and show your good fellowship by feasting with us." The Prince entered their circle and when he had sat down, they passed some portions of their grizzly feast on to him. With great skill he pretended to eat, but in reality he dropped the bones behind him. At the same time, he boasted so loudly about all his achievements and exploits that the giants never noticed what he was doing.

"And what is your name, O valiant sir?" said the leader of the giants. "I am called Nine Man Mord," replied the Prince, giving the name of a hero who had made himself famous by slaying nine enemies with one stroke.

The giants had heard of his mighty deeds and said that they were indeed grateful to have such a capable fellow joining them. They invited him to go hunting with them. The chief of the giants led the way saying, "Not far away from here is a town where we can find plenty to eat."

Soon they reached the walls of the city and the giants began to make preparations for climbing over, by pulling up two great trees and leaning one of them against the ramparts. Then the leader called out, "Nine Man Mord, as you are the lightest, you shall climb to the top first and fasten the trees, so that all will be safe for us to climb over." Without difficulty the Prince climbed the tree and then the giants pushed up the second for him to fix as a ladder on the other side.

"We are ready to go," said the Prince. One after the other, the giants climbed to the top, crossed the wall, and began to descend on the other side. But just as each giant was safely out of sight of the others down below, the Prince drew his sword and smote off his head. Then he cried out, "Your companion is safely over, come on up." Quick was their descent indeed, until finally it was the turn of the leader.

He paused for a moment at the top of the wall. "What are they doing?" he cried. But before he was able to see for himself what lay at the bottom of the tree, the Prince had severed his head too. He placed his sword back into the scabbard and, passing by the nine headless bodies of the giants, made his way to explore the city.

All the streets were dark and deserted and the houses looked as though they were falling into decay. The giants had been coming night after night in search of prey; they had brought about destruction everywhere. It was so terrible that the Czar, many months before, had issued a command that as soon as the sun set, all lights were to be extinguished, all doors locked, and no one was to walk on the streets of the city. Thus, the Prince on his early morning walk did not meet a soul.

It was strange, but after a while he saw a distant light shining from a turret window. "Here at least," thought the Prince, "is some lonely soul who is keeping watch."

He made his way in that direction and soon came to a tower with a small postern door, which was standing ajar. The Prince opened it and slowly walked up a flight of winding stairs. At the top he found a door, which led into a turret room. It was the room from which the light was shining. The Prince entered and stood amazed, as on a bed of gold lay the most beautiful maiden he had ever seen. Her hair outshone the gold in its glory and her skin was like the purest snow. He was entranced. But as he stood there, he became aware that there was another watcher in that room.

Above the bed there hung a terrible serpent with cold glittering eyes, its neck arched and its fangs ready to strike as soon as the sleeper gave the faintest stir of life. With a cry, the Prince drew his dagger. "Hold wood, hold dagger!" he shouted. "May only the true owner draw forth this blade from the wood."

With only one swift stroke he pierced the neck of the serpent, leaving it securely pinned to the wall. Then he turned around and, crossing the streets of the deserted city and climbing over the wall, he hurried back to the lakeside.

His brothers were still sleeping, but as soon as dawn was beginning to peep over the eastern hills, he roused them from their slumber. Their first question was, "Did you have a quiet watch?"

"Yes," he replied, for he too had decided not to talk about his adventures. However, he did tell them about the beautiful and strange city he had visited and then suggested that they go there together to find some food and lodging. The brothers were happy and readily agreed after so many days of travel through dark forests and sleeping on hard ground.

Soon after they were seated in a warm inn, enjoying a hot meal and toasting each other with excellent red wine. Their look of contentment attracted to their table a stranger who had been sitting by the fire. As the three young princes were easy to talk to, the stranger told them some of his most daring deeds and then asked them: "What can you tell me? You must have some exciting exploits to your names."

The eldest prince answered, "We are young and have not yet seen a great deal of the world, but three nights ago I did have an adventure. I was attacked by a great monster, which I promptly slew, and to witness the truth of my statement, here are its ears." He opened his pouch and took out the ears of the monster he killed.

"Goodness me," said the second brother. "I killed a monster with two heads and cut off four ears" and he threw them on the table.

"Well," said the youngest brother, "the monster I killed had three heads and so I cut off six ears!" All of them stared at their youngest brother because it had never occurred to them that their youngest brother could do the bravest deed.

"You are indeed valiant," said the stranger. "You must be almost as strong as the unknown hero who visited us during the night. We have had terrible problems in this town. For many months it has been attacked by terrible giants. Most of our flocks and herds have been destroyed and many people have lost their lives. Every night a few more disappeared from their homes and this morning what do you think the Czar found when he walked through the city? There, under the wall lay all the giants with their heads severed from their bodies. But this was not the only surprise he found. When he went to see his daughter, the Princess, he found that there she was sleeping so sweetly and above, pinned to the wall with a dagger, was a terrible serpent which must have been slain just as it was ready to destroy her. The dagger still stands fixed in the wall and the Czar has offered his daughter in marriage to the one who can withdraw the dagger, for he must be the true slayer of the serpent."

The young Prince now confessed that it was none other than he himself who killed the giants and the serpent.

"Let us go at once to the Czar," said the young stranger. "If you are indeed as you say, you will be able to pull forth the dagger and prove your right to the hand of the Princess."

The four left for the palace immediately, and the stranger led the way. The chamber was crowded with courtiers, all trying to lay their claim to the dagger. Of course no one could move it. The Czar at first doubted the Prince's story, but then asked each one of the young princes to try and pull out the dagger. The eldest son tried with all his might, but it did not move even a fraction of an inch. The second was equally unsuccessful. Then the third took hold of the handle and shouted: "Yield wood! Yield dagger! The true owner draws forth the blade."

With one wrench he withdrew the dagger from the wall and the snake fell to the floor. Everybody was delighted and proclaimed him the true hero who had saved the city and freed the Princess. The Prince and Princess were united in a beautiful wedding.

For some time everyone was happy, and the festivities lasted many days. When it was quiet again, the Czar offered the two elder princes castles and land if they wanted to stay in his czardom. But they still mourned for their lost sisters and so decided to go and search for them. The youngest son stayed with his wife, the Princess, in the beautiful castle.

At first he was very happy because he loved her dearly, but slowly he began to reproach himself for being contented and idle when his brothers were enduring toil and hardship looking for their three sisters. From day to day he grew more melancholic and sad, which the Czar did not fail to notice. He tried everything to cheer up his son-in-law and one day said to him, "My son, today I go forth to hunt, but as I see that you no longer enjoy the pleasures of the chase, I will ask you to guard my palace until my return." He gave him nine keys to his secret chambers.

"These chambers contain many beautiful things and they will bring you delight, for the first four rooms reveal the joys of the Earth, the next three unfold the joys of Heaven, and the eighth contains the joys of Earth and Heaven in one. But into the ninth room you must not go or great misfortune will befall us."

The Czar left on his hunt and the Prince began to explore. One by one he opened the secret rooms. In the first he found the wonders of the rocks and the stones, the shining jewels and the veins of silver and gold that hide in the heart of the Earth. In the second he saw the wonders of the flowers and trees; he felt the joy when the first leaves unfold in the spring and experienced the glory of the meadows bright with blossom and fruit. The third room showed him the strength and grace of the animal world—the swift eagle, the mighty lion and the darting fish. In the fourth he was confronted with all that man has attained in building and shaping the earth to his mind. In the fifth room he beheld the beauty of the Sun, in the sixth he entered the realm of the Moon, and in the seventh he found himself in the wide spaces where the countless stars have made their home.

Finally he stood before the ninth door. He asked himself the question, "What can be in this room that I am not worthy to behold? I have slain a monster with three heads, I have killed nine giants, and I have freed my Princess. Why may I not behold what is in this room? I am strong. This is just a test that the Czar has set for me. I must show him that I am undaunted and that I can dare all."

With that he turned the key and entered the room. But here no glory met his eyes. He was in a dark vault and near him, bound to a pillar stood a tall figure. It seemed to have the strength of the underworld in its limbs, of the mid-world in its set face, and of the heavens in its proud defiant gaze. It was chained to the pillar and to the rock with all the metals of the earth. Chains of gold encircled his breast, and its limbs were bound in fetters of iron. A silver band secured its head to the pillar, and a girdle of copper entwined its waist and was fixed to the stone wall. Far away through distant windows, remote and unattainable, the captive could behold the joys of the other rooms.

The strange being spoke to the Prince: "Young man, for the love of heaven, please bring me a drink of water from yonder fountain. For many a long year have I languished in these chains and not one drop has passed my lips."

The Prince became unsure—he had entered the chamber although it had been forbidden. Should he now commit any further acts?

The creature cried: "Only one draught of water, and I will grant thee a second life." A second life, thought the Prince to himself, is a desirable gift, so he hastened to the fountain and returned with a bowl of water. The creature drank it in one draught and seemed to grow taller and straighter.

"What is your name?" said the Prince.

"Bashtchelik, which means True Steel," was the reply. "But O Prince, one bowl of water is but little for such a strong and tall creature as I. Bring me one more bowl, I pray thee and I will grant thee yet another life." A bowl of water was a small payment for another life, so the Prince hastened to the fountain and gave Bashtchelik a second drink. It seemed that the strange being grew still taller and mightier.

In the courtyard of the castle the sounds of horses announced the return of the Czar. They had returned from the chase. The Prince was afraid to be caught in his act of disobedience, so he hastened to the door, when Bashtchelik responded to the Prince's farewell with one more request. "O noble Prince, I know thee, and I have heard of your brave deeds. Truly there is none like thee. Give me but one more drink and I will give thee a third life, for thou art worthy."

The Prince could not resist yet another life for such a small cost. He hastened to the fountain for the third drink, but even as he brought it the Czar could be heard at the gates. As Bashtchelik took the drink he and the Prince gazed at one another, and the Prince had never known a glance so compelling as that proud gaze. It seemed to him that the being grew every moment taller and stronger.

Suddenly there was a clash—the chains had fallen off, the fetters fell apart. Bashtchelik stretched himself making him taller still and as the Prince was watching, mighty wings were outspread from his shoulders. In one flash he was out the door! He swept through the passage and across the terrace. The Princess was out in the palace garden, enjoying the evening air. In full sight of the Czar, returning from his chase, Bashtchelik took the Princess and soared away over the clouds beyond their furthest sight.

"Alas!" cried the Czar, "What have you done? I lost three armies in capturing this terrible being and now that he goes forth with renewed strength, he will never be taken prisoner again."

"Do not despair," said the Prince, "I will not rest until I have found Bashtchelik and won back my bride."

"May God protect you," said the Czar, "for it is an impossible quest."

The Prince was not to be held back. He set out immediately. Everywhere looking for news of Bashtchelik, he rode through many different countries and strange lands until one day he came to a beautiful city. It was strange, the city was empty, but as he rode through the deserted streets under the great strong walls, he heard a voice calling him. In answer he dismounted and turned to enter the courtyard, when a girl came running out to meet him. With great joy, the Prince clasped her in his arms, for it was none other than his eldest sister.

"What are you doing here? How did you get here?" he asked after a while.

"This is the city where I am queen," she replied. "My husband is the Falcon King. But he is gone all day long with his army of falcons and only comes back in the evening. We have all the time we want to enjoy each other's company."

She led him to a tower and gave him food and drink more delicious than any he had tasted on his long journeys. They had so much to tell each other that the day soon passed. As evening came the air was filled with the whirring of falcon wings as the King returned. He came sweeping into the palace chamber.

The queen had quickly hidden the Prince, but the Falcon King sniffed the air. "I smell the bones of a human being," he cried.

"How can you imagine such a thing?" replied his wife. "What human being could ever reach this city?" she asked.

"My senses have never yet deceived me. It is those brothers of yours who have come to look for you."

"That is absolute nonsense. How could they ever find their way to this place?" she replied. Then the eldest sister added, "But suppose it were my eldest brother, what would you do?"

"I would tear out his eyes with my sharp beak," cried the Falcon King.

"But suppose it were my second brother?"

"I would not only tear out his eyes, but I would stew them and eat them."

"And if it were my youngest brother?"

"Ah! That would be different. Your youngest brother gave you to me in marriage, and if he were to appear, I would treat him as a true friend."

"My youngest brother is here," said the princess as she flung open the door and revealed the Prince.

"You are my true brother," said the Falcon King. "What can I do to help you?"

The Prince told his story and asked the Falcon King to help him find Bashtchelik.

"My dear brother," said the King, "I beg you to give up such an idea, for it is impossible for you to succeed. In heaven and earth there is no power that is able to overcome Bashtchelik. Forget about the past and go home to your own country. If you will abandon this idea, I will give you a horse laden with gold."

"I cannot give it up," said the Prince, "for Bashtchelik has taken away my dearly loved wife and I cannot abandon her."

"If you are determined to continue your journey," said the King, "I will give you whatever help I can. Here is a golden feather from my wing. Whenever you are in need, burn this feather and all the hosts of the falcons will fly to your aid."

The Prince was grateful and thanked his host warmly. Saying goodbye to his dear friends, he set out once more upon his quest.

He travelled through still wilder and desolate lands till among the mountains he came to a second city. Like the first it was deserted and he rode through many empty streets. After a while he heard his name being called, and like the first time, it turned out to be his sister, his second sister. She told him that she was the bride of the Eagle King, and she led him to her tower chamber where they talked all day.

At night when her husband returned with all his pinions, he swooped into the room and was immediately aware of a human being in the place. "I smell the flesh of a human being," he said.

The princess responded, "You have strange ideas. How could a human being find his way to this castle's walls?"

"I told you that I can smell what I can smell."

"You worry without reason," said his bride. "However, suppose my eldest brother did come, what would you do?"

"I would tear out his heart with my sharp beak."

"And suppose it were my second brother?"

"I would not only tear out his heart, but I would rend it into little pieces and stew them and gobble them all up."

"And what would you do about my youngest brother?"

"Ah, your youngest brother, him I would welcome with open arms. He is my true friend because he gave you to me in marriage."

The princess immediately opened the door to the hiding place and begged the youngest brother to come out. After they talked for a while and the Prince had told the King of all his adventures, he asked his advice in the case of Bashtchelik.

"There is no hope that you can overcome him," he said, and tried to dissuade him, offering him two horses laden with sacks of gold. "All you need to do is return to your own country," the Eagle King advised. Of course the Prince did not want to give up his Princess and remained adamant.

When the King saw that the Prince was determined, he gave him a golden feather from his wing. "When you are in trouble," he said, "burn this feather and I will come to your aid with all my hosts of eagles."

The next morning the Prince bade farewell and continued on his quest. His path went through an even wilder and rockier countryside than before, and at last on a lofty crag overhanging a deep ravine he came upon a mountain city. Like the others this one seemed deserted. But, again he heard his name called and, lo and behold, it was his youngest sister. "What are you doing here?" he asked, and she told him that she was the wife of the Dragon King. She led him to the castle room where they spent the day together for they had much to tell.

Towards evening the earth seemed to tremble. "It is my husband, the Dragon King, returning," said the princess. "Quickly, hide, for he does not love my brothers."

When the Dragon King entered and there was no sign of a human being, he snorted loudly and said, "I smell the blood of a human being."

"How can there be a human being here? You have travelled so far today and now you remember what you have smelled on your travels," answered his wife.

"Woman, I know what I know. It is these brothers of yours who have come to seek you."

"How could it be?" said the princess. "But supposing it were my eldest brother?"

"I would tear out his liver with my sharp talons."

"And if it were my second brother?"

"I would tear his liver into ribbons, stew every morsel until it was soft and tender and then gobble it all up."

"And if it were my youngest brother?"

"That would be completely different. He alone obeyed the wish of his dying father by allowing you to marry me. I would welcome him as a true friend."

When the Prince stepped out of his hiding place, he and the Dragon King embraced each other. But when the Prince tried to get help with Bashtchelik, the third King too tried to persuade him to let go of his goal and offered him three horses laden with sacks of gold.

The Prince's mind could not be changed. So the Dragon King also gave him a golden feather and told him that he should burn it in time of need and that he would then come to his aid with all his dragon hosts.

Then the Dragon King said to the Prince: "To reach the home of Bashtchelik, you must cross a high range of mountains and a wide plain. Beyond that there lies a mighty cave. It is the favorite haunt of this terrible being."

It was difficult for the Prince to traverse the mountain range, but after many trials he succeeded and crossed the wide plain. There was the cave in the distance and in its entrance he saw his wife. Her golden hair was shining in the sunlight. He ran forward as fast as his feet would carry him and embracing her said, "My dear, dear wife, have I found you at last? Now you can come home with me!"

The Princess seemed sad when she said, "How can I? Bashtchelik will find that I have gone and he will follow us."

"But you belong to me. You are my wife! If he pursues us, have I not four lives?"

The Prince seated her on his horse and, as swiftly as possible, they rode away. All day they travelled until, in the evening, the sun began to set. This was the time when Bashtchelik returned home from his travels. When he found the cave empty, he flew into the air with a wild shriek and with ever-widening circles he surveyed the landscape. He gazed far into the distance but could see no movement. The sun was sinking behind the hills when he saw its last rays reflecting on the golden hair of the Princess. They were riding their hardest to reach the shelter of the woods just before a large black forest.

"O merciful heaven," cried the Princess, "Bashtchelik is following us. Fly faster! Please fly faster!"

Before the Prince could leap from his horse and draw his sword, he found himself clasped in a tight grip. "Foolish Prince," said Bashtchelik in anger. "Out of gratitude I gave you three lives. One of them you have now lost. Do not tempt my anger a second time." Bashtchelik took the Princess with him and left the Prince on the wide plain.

The Prince was courageous and did not give up easily, thinking that he had two more lives, plus his own. So he attempted to fetch his Princess home a second and a third time using swifter horses, but Bashtchelik overtook him each time depriving him of two more lives. The third time the great winged being said, "Oh Prince, the three lives which I gave you out of gratitude, you have now lost. There is only your own life left. No power on earth can overcome me. Remember that."

The Prince was sad as he wondered what he could do now. He was determined not to leave his wife in the hands of Bashtchelik. Then he thought of the three golden feathers, which he had received from the Falcon, the Eagle, and the Dragon Kings. Again he went to the Princess and gave her the three feathers.

"We will flee once more," he said to her, "but this time as Bashtchelik swoops above us, I will draw my sword and you must set fire to the three feathers. Then the Falcon, Eagle, and Dragon Kings with their hosts will come to our aid. Bashtchelik will be driven away this time."

Everything happened as the Prince had predicted. As Bashtchelik appeared, the Princess set fire to the feathers and a host of falcons, eagles and dragons filled the air. The sun darkened behind a cloud of wings, and the screeching of birds was overwhelming. At last Bashtchelik retreated and the three kings claimed victory. Then they turned around and saw that, although Bashtchelik had gone, he had struck a deathblow to the Prince and taken the Princess with him.

The three kings held counsel, and the Falcon King said, "On the slopes of a distant mountain flows a spring of the Water of Life."

"We will send a messenger," said the Eagle King, "so that our brother may be brought back to life."

"My dragons will be the speediest couriers," announced the Dragon King. "They will be there and return within the speed of one heartbeat."

The dragons indeed brought the Water of Life within one heartbeat. The three kings sprinkled the water over the silent form of their brother-in-law and at once he opened his eyes and sat up. His first question was: "Where is the Princess? I must go and find her!"

"Listen!" said the three Kings. "This game makes no sense. No power on earth can overcome Bashtchelik unless we find the source of his hidden strength. You must go to the cave while Bashtchelik is gone and speak to the Princess. Only if he tells her the hidden strength of his power will we be able to overcome him. She must use all her skills and cunning to draw this secret from him. Then we will know what to do." The Prince returned to the Princess and asked her to coax the knowledge from Bashtchelik of where his hidden strength lay, for her freedom depended on it.

That night when Bashtchelik returned, the Princess appeared very loving. "Dear Bashtchelik, our life together will no longer be disturbed. You have shown yourself to be stronger than any power on earth. I love this strength of yours. Can you tell me what the source of your strength is? I would like to bind you with my hair to show you that my love is stronger than thy strength."

Bashtchelik laughed, "My strength lies in my sword! Take that away from me and I would be as weak and helpless as thy Prince!"

The Princess took the sword, set it up in a corner and began to sing a song in praise of the powerful sword that made Bashtchelik into a hero. Bashtchelik began to laugh, "You foolish woman, my strength does not lie in my sword or in my scabbard."

The Princess seemed sad. "You are making fun of me," she said downcast. "You don't believe in my love for you."

"If it is really thy wish to know, I will tell thee," said Bashtchelik. "I have a bow and arrow which are magic. That is where my strength lies."

Then the Princess began to sing praises to the swift bow and arrow. When Bashtchelik laughed even louder, she began to weep saying that he did not love her any longer. Bashtchelik wanted very much to win her love and affection, so he asked her: "Why dost thou wish to know?"

"That I may love and honor you even more!"

"Like all women, you will tell it to everyone else!"

"Whom can I tell, seeing that the Prince my husband is no longer alive? It is clear that thou dost not love me!"

Bashtchelik believed that the Prince was dead and more than anything else he wanted her love. So he said, "Not far from here rises a great and lofty mountain. Its summit reaches to the sky and its roots are planted deep into the earth. In that mountain there is a cave and in it lies a sleeping serpent. In a corner, quite close to the serpent, hides a fox. If anyone were to capture him, from his mouth would spring forth a bird, and if the bird were caught, there would leap from its beak a fish. If the fish were brought to land, from its jaws would roll an egg. In that egg lies my strength, and whosoever destroys that egg, destroys me."

Then the Princess wrapped Bashtchelik's head in her hair and sang him to sleep. "There is indeed no one like thee in strength!"

The following day the Prince learned the secret and he called his friends, the Falcon, the Eagle, and the Dragon Kings. They consulted together and decided that the Prince should hunt out the fox and then the hosts of the falcons, the eagles and the dragons would give chase together.

The Prince found the mountain whose summit went to the sky and whose roots were planted in the earth. Within its cave he found the sleeping serpent. He roused the fox and drove him out. Swift as lightning, the fox darted across the plain, but far swifter were the hosts of falcons. They attacked him from every side with their claws and sharp beaks until from its mouth started to fly a bird.

Away it went like a meteor, but it could not escape the eagle squadrons who swiftly followed after it. When they had the bird firmly in their talons, the fish leapt from its beak. Down it dove into the lake. It disappeared below the waters; however, it could not escape the dragons that plunged into the waters, where the pursuit continued. The leader of the dragons managed to catch the rolling egg that had fallen from the fish's mouth and laid it before the Prince's feet. Immediately the Prince placed his foot on the egg and crushed it. Then the kings made a great fire and threw the crushed egg into its flames. As the fire soared up, a strange sight appeared before their eyes.

Before them lay the great winged being, completely helpless. As they gazed, it changed and shrank in the searing heat until at last the flames died down, leaving only the charred wings and a burnt heart. That was the end of Bashtchelik.

The Prince and Princess were now reunited and returned to her father, the Czar, who was overjoyed to see his daughter again and hear of Bashtchelik's death. The eldest two Princes after a long and vain search, came back and heard of their youngest brother's adventures and success. They were very happy indeed at the discovery of their sisters. Thus all ended in happiness and there was no cloud to darken their future, for the great Bashtchelik was dead.

I once saw this, and if what happened in the spiritual world did not succumb to death, it must still be alive today.

The story of *The Fisher-Prince with the Silver Apple* describes an individual path of inner development towards harmony and freedom. The task is to become conscious of one's thinking, feeling, and willing and to gain strength to free the Princess from the dragon. The reader accompanies the Fisher-Prince in his silver boat into the realm where he experiences the inspiring shooting stars, where he meets the heavenly knight and receives continuous help from the golden fish. In the process of his journey, the Fisher-Prince is able to free himself from imbalances in his soul, while he steadily grows in strength. The whole story envelopes the reader in warmth, charm, beauty, and success.

When one reflects on the content of the fairy tale of *Bashtchelik or True Steel*, it is very different. It appears that this story uncovers the struggles of mankind in its darkest hours. Already in the beginning of the story, the reader is exposed to thunder, lightning, earthquakes, and soul drama through the mysterious disappearance of the three sisters. There is nothing that embraces him with beauty or protects him from experiencing these strong forces. The very foundations of the earth are stirred up by an earthquake. Out of the water comes a dragon, not a golden fish. Instead of young animals in need of care, the reader faces the King of the Eagles, the King of the Falcons and the King of the Dragons. He gets to know all three as cruel in their response to the older brothers. The young Prince himself enters into states of loneliness, repeated defeat and death. In spite of all these incredible hurdles, he finds his sisters and in the end wins back his Princess and is reunited with his brothers! This is possible only because he has the necessary soul characteristics: perseverance, determination, and courage. These help him on his difficult path and never leave him throughout the story.

It is interesting that the Prince remains nameless. Perhaps it indicates that he could bear the name of any human being, be any one of us, and that in fact, he is quite ordinary in spite of being a Prince.

Faith, Love, and Hope

In the beginning of the story, the youngest Prince finds himself in a situation where his father, the dying Czar, demands of him and his brothers that they give their three sisters in marriage to whoever asks for them. When the elements rage and the suitors appear, the three brothers are in the castle together with everyone else. Each time, the two older brothers are overwhelmed, full of fear and unwilling to let the sisters go, but not so the youngest. The youngest Prince is very different from his brothers. He alone is confident and fearless. Without hesitation he obeys the command of his father.

Firmly he declares, "Though the heavens threaten us, I will obey him"—and he is convinced that his obedience protects him. The youngest Prince does not have to fear anything because he believes in his father. In fact he asks his brothers, "What have we to fear?" He alone is convinced that disobedience of his father's command will lead to punishment.

This points to an ancient time when mankind obeyed the laws laid down for them by their spiritual leaders. When Moses brought the Ten Commandments to the Hebrew people, those laws were obeyed out of fear of punishment. The God of the Old Testament appeared as a strong and dominating force.

In the fairy tale, the Prince says, "Terrible punishment falls on those who disobey the wishes of the dying," and then goes on to say, "It is not for fear of punishment, but because I loved our father that I wish to carry out his last command." When one studies these words of the youngest son more closely, they point to a bridge from the Old to the New Testament, which embraces love as the foundation of Christianity.

As the future unfolds, it will embrace a time when conscience alone dictates behavior, and when love alone will lie at its foundation. One can see in the youngest Prince's faith that his father's command serves the good. He loves him and hopes that he will find his sisters again, knowing that they cannot be lost. Faith, love, and hope, virtues that were pointed out by Paul in his Epistle to the Corinthians[2] are deeply interwoven in this fairy tale. An initiation path without these virtues is unthinkable. All three have to rise to full consciousness in the youngest Prince. Their loss at the beginning of the story is no coincidence.

Talking about these three virtues, Rudolf Steiner said in his lecture "Faith, Love and Hope: On the Third Revelation":

> It is precisely in physical life that we need hope, for everything is upheld by hope and without it nothing can be done. The forces of hope, therefore, are connected with our last sheath as human beings, with our physical body. What the forces of faith are for our astral body, and the love-forces for the etheric, the forces of hope are for the

physical body. …Faith, love, hope, constitute three stages in the essential being of man; they are necessary for health and for life as a whole, for without them we cannot exist. Just as work cannot be done in a dark room until light is obtained, it is equally impossible for a human being to carry on in his fourfold nature if his three sheaths are not permeated, warmed through, and strengthened by faith, love, and hope.

Physical and Moral Strength

Revealing indications can be found in Rudolf Steiner's fairy tale lecture regarding giants and sisters, as well as wise female beings.[3] When people are in their physical bodies, he said, they perceive the world around them with their physical organs of perception. Behind that, however, is the spiritual world.

Everything that man once perceived clairvoyantly in the spiritual world had at one time been a part of his innermost self. In Rudolf Steiner's own words: "When the outer senses are silenced, the soul comes to life. …The figures that thus appeared to him were facsimiles of his own figure—men of immense strength. These are the 'giants.' The giants are stupid, because they belong to a time when man could not use the intellectual soul; they are strong, but stupid."[4]

Rudolf Steiner also described that long ago mankind was very close to the forces of nature and to supersensible beings. He was able to command the elements, and because he had a very strong life force or etheric body, he also had incredible strength. Man could pull up trees, as so often happens in fairy tales. At that time he also had strong feelings, while his capacity to think had not yet developed. Although fairy tales were inspired during the last few centuries, nevertheless they contain past experiences, as was pointed out.

69
The Kiss of Death
Hans Baldung
(1480–1545)

In the story of *Bashtchelik*, the youngest brother knows that he cannot fight the giants in the same way in which he had fought the dragons. He is greatly outnumbered, and they are much stronger. Instead, he uses his capacity to think and decides to separate and kill them by outwitting them. Clever and cunning heroes who overcome giants are depicted not only in fairy tales but also in the Bible, as in David and Goliath.[5] Another well-known example is found in Homer's epic poem *The Odyssey*, in which Odysseus overcomes the Cyclops.

The giants, as we see them in *Bashtchelik or True Steel* are eating bones, the deadest part of the human body. Rudolf Steiner asserts that man has become entangled in the mineral part of the earth. He has incorporated into himself solid bony substance. He goes on to say: "Death came to him [man] because of this, and it is not without cause that death is represented by a skeleton."[6] The taking up of mineral substance from the earth in order to build the body could well be represented as the giants eating bones. Their action also emphasizes the lack of intelligence. To overcome death and to enter into a new, more conscious life is the goal of the Prince's journey. The marriage of the Prince to the Princess, when it finally occurs, celebrates this step. It is not difficult to find representations of the skeleton in connection with death in the world of art: *The Kiss of Death* by Hans Baldung (illustration 69) and A. Koburger's humorous drawing depicted in *The Dance of Death* (illustration 70) may serve as examples.

The heroes in fairy tales often encounter challenges and struggles that they must overcome. This may remind the reader of life situations that may seem difficult at the outset but can be overcome after several trials. In this fairy tale, the first dragon has one head, the next two, and the third, which was overcome by the youngest Prince, had three heads; the final struggle, of course, needed the greatest strength. Every fairy tale lover knows that it is usually the third attempt which proves successful. Often it is also the third of three princes or heroes who wins the final battle.

70

The Dance of Death, A. Koburger, 15th c.

In *Bashtchelik*, the two older brothers are in fact imaginations that describe the youngest Prince. They represent the youngest Prince's previous struggles to overcome evil when he had yet to acquire his spiritual strength. The three brothers are actually one; they are the youngest Prince.

Why is it that human beings are repeatedly presented with challenges? Rudolf Steiner explained, "Now suppose that you have to push a cart. You develop your strength through pushing it. If it were more heavily loaded, you would have to push harder, but as a result you would also develop greater strength. Humanity, however, could be made stronger by having obstacles put in its path."[7]

The theme of acquiring strength weaves through this fairy tale and if perceived from a more spiritual viewpoint, it may be said that a loving father will test his son at each stage of development, as did Prince Ivan's in *The Firebird*. The father determines whether the Prince is strong enough to take the next step on the path of initiation. A student that follows the path of initiation develops the consciousness that allows him or her to clairvoyantly experience the higher world. Not only does this world consist of harmony and beauty, but also of negative forces. Here, strength of ego and character are certainly required. Of course the insight of an initiate goes far beyond the possibilities of an ordinary human being, and Rudolf Steiner explains that "an initiation event is nothing other than man's gaining the capacity of developing organs of vision in his higher bodies. Today man sees darkness when it is night; he is in the dark. This is because man has no organs of perception in his astral body. As the eyes and ears have formed themselves into physical organs of perception, so super-sensible organs must be developed out of the higher members and assimilated into them. This occurs through certain exercises of concentration and meditation being given to the pupil."[8] Anyone may attempt the path of initiation. Rudolf Steiner pointed out that a teacher will find the student when he or she is ready.

Searching for the Self and Conquering Fears

The path of the youngest Prince does not evolve as in other fairy tales in which the Prince sets out to search for, rescue, or win his Princess. In this story, he neither knows her nor has he heard of her when he sets out on his journey. Rather, he and his two older brothers set out to search for their three sisters.

For the youngest Prince one may say that he is searching for a higher sisterly nature comprised of character traits that live unconsciously within everyone. Faith, love, and hope were mentioned earlier as possibilities. He will find these traits only when he commits himself to fearlessly finding Bashtchelik through his own free will. It is interesting to note that while the Prince was searching for his sisters, he found his Princess. Later, when he searches for his Princess, he finds his sisters and receives nourishment, strength, and help from them. Could the sisters indeed represent faith, love, and hope? As each sister finds the Prince, these qualities become fully conscious in him. He enjoys their benefit, as he continues his search for the Princess.

The story of Bashtchelik emphasizes the necessity of gaining strength by overcoming fear on many different levels. Each of the three suitors, or kings, appears as a different element in his approach to the castle. The King of the Falcons approaches with thunder and flashes of lightning in the sky. Through his penetrating sight he represents a higher sphere and clairvoyant capacity. The Eagle King appears as a mighty wind from the middle sphere, which rattles the doors between heaven and earth. Confronted by such a powerful force and accompanied by a palpitating heart, courage can quickly fail. The Dragon King shakes life forces to the core as he instills fear through an earthquake—"the very foundations of the earth seemed to rock and from the rumbling of the deep came a mighty voice."

These events are designed to show that the Prince is being challenged by nature and its powerful forces. The two older brothers are overcome with fear, mistrust, and horror at the thought of giving away their sisters. Later in the story, their weaknesses called forth the hostility of the kings. The Falcon King sees the fear and mistrust that live within the lesser-developed eldest brother. These weaknesses prevent him from clearly seeing and understanding the situation. The following references to the eyes can be found in the Gospel according to St. Matthew, "The light of the body is the eye. …But if thine eye be evil, thine whole body shall be full of darkness."[9]

The Eagle King represents the middle sphere, the sphere of the heart. The second brother, when confronted by the elements, loses his courage. He becomes fearful and weak. The Eagle King perceives his weakness and wants to tear out his heart, cut it into small pieces and gobble it up. In its present state, the second brother's heart is too weak for spiritual progress. It needs to be taken out, cut into little pieces, stewed, and digested. This implies that the heart needs to be carefully examined.

The heart and its connection to love and the soul are cherished by all people. Vladimir Soloviev, a mystic, philosopher, and poet writes about the heart: "The most important organ of man is the heart—not the physical but the spiritual heart. The abyss of the spiritual heart encompasses and includes everything. …It is the real man."[10]

The liver is the very foundation of our physical existence. It is known as the organ of life because of its ability to regenerate.[11] Both in English and in the German languages, the word *liver* is connected to *life* or to *living, Leber* ('liver'), *Leben* ('life').

If the eldest brother represents the development of inner sight, the middle brother then represents the development of the heart forces. The youngest brother, the Prince, represents a combination of those developed organs as well as the attribute of will. These three organs correspond to the upper, middle, and lower aspects of the human being: thinking, feeling (thinking with the heart), and willing. The danger that the two elder brothers face as a consequence of their lack of faith and love for their father, is that they lose the possibility to transform their three organs. In order to progress on the path, one has to remain open to all that presents itself to one's being.

The Archangel Michael, Lucifer and Ahriman

On his path the Prince also meets different evil forces that are connected to the evolution of mankind—evil on a wider scale. In the words of Rudolf Steiner: "Whenever something evil appears which has to be overcome, but which has remained stationary, on the astral plane, it always appears as a dragon or similar being; this is none other than the grotesque form, changed in the spiritual world, of that which man had to change and throw out of himself."[12] The dragons appear out of the water, the giants live in the cave (earth), and the serpent appears hanging in the air above the Princess's bed.

One can consider the dragon and the serpent, represented throughout art history, as being related to evil influences. These influences seek to tempt the human soul during his sojourn on earth. The snake and the dragon have been depicted for centuries in sculpture, painting, and literature. In European art they appear mostly in connection with the Archangel Michael and in Russia with his representative on earth, St. George.

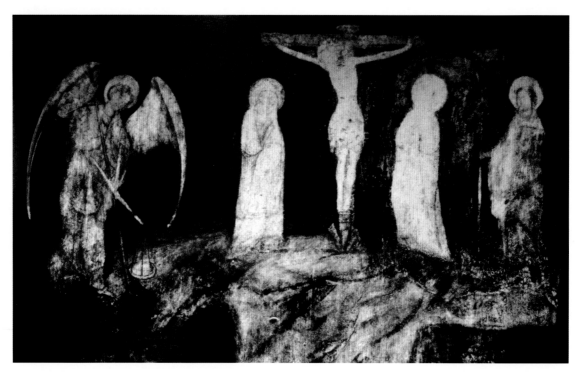

71

The Archangel Michael and Golgotha, Holland, 11th c.

In the fairy tale of *The Fisher-Prince*, the reader was introduced to the Archangel Michael, the Heavenly Knight. This Heavenly Knight truly helps the human being to forge a sword of heavenly iron for the fight against evil. As the leading Sun Archangel, the Heavenly Knight stood close to the Christ at the crucifixion on Golgotha. This is shown in *The Archangel Michael and Golgotha* (illustration 71), from a wall painting in Holland.

St. Michael is known in anthroposophy as the countenance of the Christ. This relationship connects him deeply with humanity's path and the destiny of our planet Earth. In The Revelation of St. John the Divine (12:1–9, 13:7) one can read about Michael's battle with evil and how he casts the dragon out of heaven and onto the earth. This spiritual truth is reflected in *St. Michael and the Dragon*, from *Les Très Riches Heures*, printed in the fifteenth-century book of paintings created for the Duke of Berry (illustration 72). It is assumed that it was painted by Jean Colombe in France around 1485.

Anthroposophy speaks of Lucifer and Ahriman as two major evil beings.[13] These beings are well-known throughout history. Lucifer causes a human being to detach himself from the earthly realm; he inspires illusion, pride, and fancifulness. His characteristics among others are arrogance, ambition, elusiveness and fanaticism.

72
St. Michael and the Dragon from *Les Très Riches Heures*
France, 15th c.

As a spirit being represented by the serpent, Lucifer is depicted in the painting of *The Serpent of the Garden of Eden* (illustration 73). A slithering and sliding serpent is connected to the realm of feeling. One can observe the uncomfortable and strong emotional reaction most people experience when they face a snake; it is very different from the ability to think rationally.

Between the tenth and fourteenth centuries Lucifer was depicted as a serpent. At that time man had not yet developed his ability to think as we do today. He still lived more in his feeling life. Therefore, the earliest artistic expressions of Lucifer show Michael with his foot on the serpent, as in illustration 74 from Monte Gargano, Italy.

74 *Michael and the Serpent*
Monte Gargano, Italy, 10th c.

As man became more and more connected to the earthy realm, his thinking activity began to reflect the material world around him. This slowly fostered interest in the physical and material aspects of his existence, resulting in the diminishing of thoughts related to the spiritual world. If this earthly direction continues into the future, it will eventually bypass man's true core as a spirit being.

In art it is often expressed as St. Michael or St. George fighting the dragon and no longer the serpent. In a fifteenth century painting by Ambrogio Lorenzetti, a transition can be found in a depiction of Michael fighting a serpent-like dragon (illustration 75). The multi-headed dragon is reminiscent of the dragons that rise up from the water in this fairy tale.

75
The Holy Archangel Michael
Ambrogio Lorenzetti
(1290–1348)

A more contemporary dragon creature, the dragon of Wantley, is portrayed in the illustration of a seventeenth-century English legend (illustration 76). This scaly dragon now has claws and large wings, a further step in its development.

The serpent in the Garden of Eden evolved over the centuries into the multi-headed dragon, and later still into the scaly dragon with wings. This parallels man's development from a heart-felt connection to the spirit world to one devoid of spiritual thought.

The name of the spirit being that lives in the representation of the dragon is Ahriman. He appears in ancient Persian literature as an evil spirit being who was in opposition to the God of Light, Ahura Mazdao. Biblically he is known as Satan and must be differentiated from Lucifer who is known as the Devil. What Ahriman fosters in mankind is coldness, hardness, narrow-mindedness, indolence, and pedantry. He also fosters abstract reasoning and dry materialism.

Ahriman tries to chain the human being to the earth in an attempt to exclude all spiritual realities. He hopes to turn our earth into a hard, cold place, devoid of beauty and life energies. The very fact that man is regarded as a machine by certain intellectuals is ahrimanic. The root cause of a society's ills can normally be found in its adherence to materialistic ideas.

76
The Dragon of Wantley, England

77

*St. Michael Weighing the Souls,
Surrounded by Trumpeting
Angels*
ca. 1445–1450
Rogier van der Weyden
(1399/1400–1464)

Every human being has been given free will to either pursue a solely materialistic life or to develop a healthy interest in the spirit. Michael holds the scale in order to weigh the value of all human souls. This is shown in *St. Michael Weighing the Souls, Surrounded by Trumpeting Angels* by Rogier van der Weyden (illustration 77).

In this fairy tale, the Prince easily recognizes all the evil forces that present themselves to him: the dragon threatening to swallow him, the giants eating human bones, and the snake that hung above the Princess. But in regard to Bashtchelik, the Prince is blind. He does not see his evil side because he is so much more powerful than the other evil beings. He has the strength of the underworld in his limbs, of the mid-world in his set face, and of the heavens in his proud defiant gaze.

Bashtchelik is held captive by chains made from all the metals of the earth. Later in the fairy tale, the Princess learns that Bashtchelik's power lies in a cave in a mountain whose summit reaches the sky and whose roots lie deep in the earth.

Within the cave there is a serpent. In a corner close to the serpent hides a fox. If anyone were to capture it, from its mouth would spring forth a bird. If the bird were caught, there would leap from its beak a fish. If the fish were brought to land, from its jaws would roll an egg. In the egg lies Bashtchelik's strength. And if the egg is destroyed, so is Bashtchelik.

To begin with, Bashtchelik appears before the Prince as weak and chained, and the Prince enjoys being praised by him. Our hero has become vulnerable, and, of course, this evil being knows very well how to talk to him. He pleads with him to give him more and more water. Until the very last moment the Prince is still free to escape the danger that is confronting him. The situation intensifies when he hears the Czar's arrival at the castle gate. The Prince has one last chance to find himself. There lives in him a trace of greed. He gave the drinks not out of compassion but as an exchange for extra lives. He satisfies the thirst of the evil being Bashtchelik and thereby strengthens him. The price is high, for the Prince loses his Princess. He has arrived at a point where further transformation and renewal will have to take place. He has to search for and win his Princess.

In Eastern culture the dragon has been worshipped for centuries. This can be found in Vietnamese art. Illustration 78 shows two dragons pursuing a giant pearl created by interlocking symbols of Yin and Yang, while illustration 79 is of an imperial Chinese dragon of the Ch'ing Dynasty, embroidered on a mandarin's robe. It is characterized by fire claws. The head is separate from the body, depicting its spiritual nature. Its compelling facial expression reminds one of the moment when the Prince gives the third drink to Bashtchelik and is confronted by his expanding monstrous figure and compelling glance.

Lucifer and Ahriman have their own separate domains and their own relationships with the human being. Despite their differences, they do work together. These two opposing forces of Ahriman and Lucifer try to pull the human being into one or the other direction. They are held in balance only by Him who leads the human being in a harmonious way along the right path of human development. This is the *Representative of Man* as created by Rudolf Steiner at the Goetheanum in Dornach (illustration 80). This wooden sculpture shows a human being who understands what St. Paul came to know—that only the Christ within us can deal with these very strong spiritual forces. In his words, "I am crucified with Christ: nevertheless I live; yet not I, but Christ liveth in me."[14]

78
The interlocking symbols of Yin and Yang pursued by two dragons, 18th c., Vietnam

79
Imperial dragon on a Mandarin robe
China

80
Representative of Man
1922
Rudolf Steiner
Switzerland

Through the strength of the Christ Ego working in man, he is able to recognize and control these two major cosmic forces of Ahriman and Lucifer within himself and in his social environment. He who masters them will eventually stand before humanity as a representative and follower of the Christ.

Is this the path of the Prince? Does he have to overcome the different kinds of evil and eventually the Bashtchelik in himself, in order for him to remain forever connected to his Princess?

The world of art leads us one step further; the picture is not yet complete. When Rudolf Steiner was asked where the dragon was on the earth, he answered, "Anywhere, wherever there was man on earth. That's where he was." Also, "He must henceforth continue the struggle within human nature. … The outer cosmic conflict of Michael and the Dragon was transferred to the inner human being, because only in human nature could the dragon now find his sphere of action."[15]

In the past the image of the dragon represented the power of Ahriman. Now Ahriman can be found working within each human being. Hence he is now represented as an evil human being. In the same way Bashtchelik represents Ahriman in this story.

From the Lucifer serpent in the Garden of Eden to the multi-headed serpent, the winged dragon, the scaly dragon and to Ahriman working within the human being, this has been the progression of evil in mankind. Luca Giordano's painting, *St. Michael the Archangel* (illustration 81), showing Michael subduing Ahriman, is just one of many artistic renditions depicting the fight of good and evil within the human being.

81
St. Michael the Archangel
ca. 1663
Luca Giordano

In the fairy tale of the *Fisher-Prince and the Silver Apple,* the Fisher-Prince had to first find the Heavenly Knight. When he found him, he was given a new task—to transform the three creatures which he had taken along as his companions. This is a depiction of a possible divine guidance the human being may have, to begin to transform his thinking, feeling, and willing. As a result of this, his soul becomes harmonized.

In reality the Archangel Michael waits until human beings take the first step and come to him. He is silent until there is a conscious attempt to approach the spiritual world through inner discipline and spiritual exercises, not through prayer alone. Michael is ready to help man in his fight against Ahriman. He is deeply concerned for humanity and its future. For centuries man has known that he may turn to Michael, as he cannot fight evil on his own. Therefore this has inspired him to create many beautiful paintings and sculptures of Michael. Mankind encounters evil in many different forms and Michael stands by its side.

In the dramatic fairy tale of Bashtchelik there is no representation of either the angelic world or of the Archangel Michael. However, the Prince attains to his higher self, the Princess. This is achieved through fearlessness, determination, inner strength, and the help of his sisters and the three kings of the elements. There are paths that can be found, but success is only possible if selfless love and compassion are among one's guiding lights.

After the Prince conquers the dragon with the three heads, he finds a cave where he meets the giants. Fear strikes him, but he knows that he must boldly step into their midst. It is Ahriman who creates fear in the human soul. Being conscious of this fact helps to disperse fear.

The Need for Courage and Humility

It is known in Spiritual Science that death itself is a result of the interference of evil forces in human evolution. Ahriman's ability to create fear in the human soul is reflected in man's fear of death.

In today's materialistically-oriented world, humanity is exposed to dangers and catastrophes which create fear. Fear can arise as a result of a worldwide erosion of old values leading to social insecurities. The lack of belief in the protection and guidance provided by hierarchical beings is widespread. It is just this fear that finds its way into the soul as lack of faith and diminished hope in God and man.

It is precisely through fear that a space opens in the soul where Ahriman, represented in this fairy tale by Bashtchelik, can enter ever more deeply. It is no coincidence that the fairy tale stresses the meaning of fearlessness. It is the lack of fear that distinguishes the Prince from his brothers.

Each encounter and struggle with evil forces was a step in the young Prince's development. He was able to overcome much and deserved the Princess in marriage. Through this union with the Princess, the Prince was allowed to experience the treasures of heaven and earth: the wonders of rocks and stones, the beauty of the flowers and trees, and the grace and strength of the animal world. He observed the swift eagle in the element of air, the mighty dragon connected to the element of the earth and the darting fish in the element of water. He also beheld the glorious beauty of the sun, moon, and stars.

Unlike many other fairy tales, this tale does not end with wedding bells. Those joyous moments only conclude the first part of the story. The second part brings with it darkness, cold, and imprisonment. One reads of a vault and a tall figure bound to a pillar with chains made from all the metals of the earth and a mountain cave with a large sleeping serpent. One can well ask, "Why does life become so challenging for the Prince?"

The Czar asked the Prince to look after the castle, allowing him to enter all the chambers except for the ninth one. The moment he stood before the locked door of the ninth chamber is clearly described in the fairy tale. "Am I not worthy to behold?" he asks. "Have I not slain the three-headed monster? Have I not saved the life of the Princess?" The Prince remembers all his deeds and is proud of them and rationalizes that the czar only wants to test him. His humility and obedience have been lost. With pride entering his soul he loses his wakefulness and faces the greatest danger, that of losing his precious Princess. Unaware of his potential loss, he steps into the ninth chamber in all his glory and happiness. The evil being which confronts him with a compelling, arrogant gaze, is Bashtchelik, who demands from him a drink of water in return for another life.

The Prince did not have to look for his Princess; she was given to him by the King as a reward for his bravery and courage. The Princess was not won by his own conscious achievement. As a result, after marrying the Princess, a unification with his higher self, other character weaknesses were revealed. In order to keep his Princess, the overcoming of his own vanity, pride and egoism must be achieved.

When one looks at this fairy tale as a mirror of society, it is easy to identify with the plight of the Prince. The evil Bashtchelik is active everywhere, while the good Princess remains hidden. At this halfway mark of the story, the hero comes to a turning point in his destiny and begins with a new conscious decision—to look for his Princess and overcome Bashtchelik.

The Firebird dealt with the development of the will and the Fisher-Prince with the transformation of the three human soul forces. In *Bashtchelik or True Steel*, however, one witnesses an independent and conscious effort to fight evil. In this fairy tale one meets a Prince, who in spite of his yet undiscovered weaknesses, may move forward due to his perseverance and courage.

Newly-Awakened Consciousness

True fairy tales have important messages to reveal. In this story, the Prince is strong and clever. He overcomes dragons, giants and a serpent, marries a Princess and lives in a castle with all the treasures of heaven and earth. Although he has all these riches, he may not settle down and be satisfied with his achievements. Having witnessed the power of Bashtchelik, he must remain awake and humble at all times. Experiencing the loss of his Princess, he realizes that the possibility of losing what he has gained is always present. It is this continuous wakefulness that is the mark of a conscious soul. In this regard, it is no coincidence that Rudolf Steiner called our time the Age of the Consciousness Soul.

At the beginning of the story the Prince was not conscious of what the three kings of the elements represented. While he acted out of obedience to his father's wishes, the kings were unknown forces to him. He had neither questions nor thoughts about the events. He simply acted out of love and loyalty. Later in the story, this changes when he meets the three kings in their own kingdoms. From the Falcon King he gains the capacity for greater vision, from the Eagle King the need for a conscious understanding of love and compassion, and from the Dragon King the realization that the Water of Life is sacred. There are no human beings visible in their kingdoms and the cities are uninhabited. This indicates to the reader that this imagination is a soul experience, open only to the searching and questioning individual. The empty and lonely streets reveal the Prince's soul condition. Suddenly his oldest sister appears and calls out his name. She is still young. This may be interpreted as meaning that a soul virtue remains always young. Indeed, in himself he discovers a soul condition that was only hidden, or in fairy tale language, his sister was never really lost. His sister was even protected by "the great strong walls" of the city.

The good virtues, represented by his sisters whom the Prince gave away to the three kings at the beginning of the story, are now rediscovered in full consciousness. Each of his sisters calls out to the brother and he recognizes each one. At the beginning of the story the Prince set out to seek his sisters in faith, love, and hope, although an understanding of these virtues remained hidden to him. As he becomes conscious of the virtues, the sisters one by one recognize him and call out his name.

In his lecture on "The Interpretation of Fairy Tales," Rudolf Steiner shares with us what takes place in a human being, "When people are in their physical bodies, they perceive the world around them with their physical organs of perception; but behind that is the spiritual world. In these intermediate states it was as if a veil were lifted from man (the veil of the physical world), and the spiritual world became visible; everything that was in the spiritual world stood related to that which was in the innermost of man. …When the outer senses are silenced the soul comes to life." He then goes on to say, "What I see there as the wise female beings is something really related to me."[16]

The external senses are silent in such intermediate states, while that which lives within the soul becomes active. Therefore, one can understand the imagination of sisters arising when these female beings appear. The time will come when out of necessity every human being will consciously rediscover the good that at one time or another lived in his soul and struggles to be reborn.

The Falcon King recognizes the Prince through the smell of human bones; the Eagle King through the smell of flesh, and the Dragon King through the smell of blood. This is a progression from the hardened to the living, from the bone to the blood. Rudolf Steiner pointed out that, "whereas in our blood we are alive, we are in our bony system, strictly speaking, already dead. … Our bony system is like a scaffolding, the thing in us that is least of all alive, only a scaffolding to support us."[17]

As was already mentioned, the blood is connected to the human ego, the "I Am." We know from Spiritual Science that "as the fourth principle of his being man has an ego, and that as this develops, the blood is its outer physical instrument."[18] It might be said that on his long and arduous path, the Prince strengthened and enlivened his ego forces, which the Dragon King was able to recognize. The fairy tale speaks of the blood instead of the ego, although these two are closely related. The Prince was given food by two of his sisters, more delicious than he had eaten on his travels. They took him to their towers. The tower in the fairy tale is an imagination for the human head with which one associates the faculty of thinking. It is likely that the food was spiritual nourishment— inspired thinking. Thoughts lacking spirituality can be compared to bones. While in this story the Prince received spiritual food from the first two kingdoms, by the king of the third kingdom he was given the Water of Life. The Dragon King himself brought it to him. Thus the Prince was given sustenance and protection without which no pupil can progress on a spiritual path.

The Prince was unable to keep his Princess because he had not yet developed the strength that he needed. For this reason he is tested again and again by the three Kings. They try to convince him that it does not make sense to pursue his quest of winning the Princess, that no power on earth can overcome Bashtchelik. The Prince, however, shows new courage, selflessness and determination. Neither doubt nor gold can deter him from his path. He repeatedly declines the offers of horses laden with sacks full of gold, meaning that he has overcome greed in himself. He courageously continues on his path with a clear vision, a loving heart and the spiritual strength bestowed on him.

Before the Prince can finally overcome Bashtchelik, he has to lose everything given to him as a reward for his weaknesses of vanity, greed, and pride. The three lives he had gained were taken back by Bashtchelik. As long as he was under Bashtchelik's power, his fight to win the Princess was unsuccessful. Only when he lost those gifts, given by this evil being, was he free to take the final step. He goes through a death and resurrection experience. In the old initiation mysteries a highly developed student or neophyte was led as a last step into a death experience, through which he could attain a new level of consciousness. During his time in the spiritual world, such a pupil attained higher mystery knowledge.[19] Similarly in our story, the Prince is given the secret knowledge of how to overcome and destroy Bashtchelik, only after the Prince's death and resurrection.

In two of the fairy tales in this book, the main evil characters were said to be so fierce that no one could overcome them. Both Kostchei in *The Firebird*, and Bashtchelik were said to be deathless. Yet, in both stories these evil beings were overcome by the discovery of the whereabouts of their power. Ignorance breeds fear. Spiritual knowledge is the only way to triumph over evil, and anthroposophy serves this very important task for today's humanity. One may not forget the fact that these powers work through the human being. Their plans for the earth oppose those of the divine beings.

In the fairy tale of *The Crystal Ball and the Silver Saucer,* as well as in the present one, the Water of Life is used as the remedy for the return to life. Christianity is the mystery of life and death. According to Rudolf Steiner the Mystery of Golgotha was fulfilled. It entered the evolution so that new life might spring from death or, in other words, "that the living spirit might be born from our present death-related consciousness."[20] Many different mythologies depict the imagination of a resurrected God. Dionysus in Greek mythology and Osiris in Egyptian mythology are just two examples. They are symbols of what later became a reality through Christ's Deed. As a result of Christ's unification with death, "death became a well-spring of new life, of a new sun."[21]

In the future man will awaken again to perceive the cosmic forces that sustain all life in nature. When the seer observes nature, he sees elemental beings weaving through it. Freeing the beings of nature is accomplished by observing nature's beauty with wonder and reverence. Because man has lost the ability to be humble, he has also lost respect for nature. These beings yearn for man's attention and love.

There is a further insight into the realm of nature presented in this fairy tale. The three creatures: the fox, the bird, and the fish are connected to the earth, air, and water. They carry within them the black egg. These elements of earth, air, and water are also present in man: the earthly, or solid; the watery, or fluid; and the airy, or gaseous elements. In order to destroy Bashtchelik, the Prince has to crush the egg. By doing this, he places his ego in the service of the hierarchical beings.

One would assume that it is enough to crush the egg in order to cause the death of Bashtchelik. But now, at the end of the story, the fourth element, fire, appears. The Kings burn the egg in the fire. The Firebird also carried the black egg within itself. It too was burnt, purified and resurrected as a symbol of a final overcoming of evil.

Fire is a special element, differing from the other three elements. It has a two-fold nature, an inner and an outer aspect. In Chinese culture it is known that the dragon fears fire. "Dragon fire and human fire are opposite. If dragon fire comes into contact with wetness, it flames, and if it meets water, it burns. If one drives it away by means of fire, it stops burning and its flames are extinguished."[22] What does this sentence mean? The dragon fire is evil, the human fire activated by the will becomes divine. When the soul is 'wet' or lame, the dragon fire flames. When the soul is like water, meaning 'alive,' the dragon fire burns. If the soul drives it away by means of divine fire, through an activated will, the dragon fire stops burning and its flames are extinguished. Evil has no place any more. One can also say that Divine fire purifies by burning evil. It is also the fire which

82
Praying Madonna
ca. 1200
Sinai

forges the sword that is used in the fight against evil. The egg, once burnt in the purifying fire, is of no danger.

Why does the evil egg have to be burnt? What happens to an object consumed by fire? The production of light is the outcome of combustion. Mysteriously the burning of evil is transformed into light. The evil egg must be burnt in the fire, hence light is produced. This profound truth is found in the knowledge given to us by Rudolf Steiner. Evil can be purified and redeemed, and fire can be the creative power of inspiration or the destructive power of the fire-spewing dragon. This fact is spoken about in anthroposophy.[23] It takes place through Him who says, "I am the Light" and who brings baptism to humanity through fire.[24]

When the light that streams down from the cosmos is united with the light which the human being creates within himself, then evil will be redeemed and the world may be purified. Since the beginning of humanity, the path to this goal has been protected and guided by highly evolved

173

spirit beings. This has helped mankind to evolve. Human beings have developed sufficient strength and ability to decide on their own which path they will follow. We have the freedom to accept or reject spiritual development and knowledge. In his book *Macrocosm and Microcosm*, Rudolf Steiner wrote, "Those Cosmic Powers have from the beginning of human existence counted upon the expectation that light will also stream upwards from human life itself to the light that streams down from above. The Cosmic Powers have no inexhaustible reservoir of light; their reservoir is one from which the stream of forces will constantly diminish unless from human life itself, through efforts to transform thinking, feeling, and willing and to rise into the higher worlds, fresh forces, new light, were to flow back into the great reservoir of Cosmic Light and Cosmic Feeling. We are now living in the epoch when it is essential for men to be conscious that they must not merely rely upon what flows into them from Cosmic Powers but must themselves cooperate in the process of world-evolution."[25]

When one explores the hidden meanings of characters and events so creatively portrayed in fairy tales and in works of art, one discovers the creative divine guidance that protects humanity and world evolution. A treasure chest of profound spiritual truths lies hidden in literature and in the arts found in all civilizations.

It may be fitting to conclude the exploration of this fairy tale with a Russian icon of the *Praying Madonna* (illustration 82, previous page). Three stars are depicted on Mary, the mother of God. One is on the forehead and two are on the chest. The Holy Mother represents not only physical purity but also purity of the soul. These stars point to the greatness of this very special Being who lived during the time of Christ. They also represent a far distant future and the completion of humanity's path on planet Earth. This motif is depicted in many Eastern icons. When in the future, thinking, feeling and willing are transformed, man will have created what is called the Golden Triangle.

The Trinity can be found within each human being. This carries the essence of the past, manifests in the present, and creates the possibility for the future. Could this be better portrayed than in *The Trinity*? (illustration 83) It is a fifteenth-century painting found in St. Peter's Church, Basel, Switzerland.

What lies ahead for the development of the human being? Anthroposophy teaches that the astral body will transform into Spirit Self, or in Eastern terminology Mani; the etheric body will transform into Life Spirit, or Buddhi; and in the far distant future the physical body will become Spirit Man, or Atma.

To transform the soul and at the same time our planet Earth, each individual human being has to consciously develop strength of will, clarity of thinking, and heart-felt feeling. In most fairy tales these qualities are portrayed as a guide for humanity in ever-evolving and creative ways.

83
The Trinity
Switzerland
15th c.

Endnotes and Illustrations

1. Little Red Riding Hood

Endnotes

1. Anthroposophy is derived from the Greek word *anthropos* meaning 'man,' and *sophia* meaning 'wisdom.' Rudolf Steiner preferred the meaning to be understood as 'awareness of one's humanity.' Anthroposophy is a Spiritual Science that investigates the laws of the spiritual world, unfolds the old mystery wisdom, and explains world evolution and its future. Its aim is to reunite the three cultural streams that separated following the Renaissance: art, science, and religion. Through Spiritual Scientific insights, anthroposophy leads the human being to a new understanding of man and the universe. In 1924 Rudolf Steiner founded the General Anthroposophical Society, which today has branches throughout the world.

2. Rudolf Steiner, philosopher, scientist, and educator (1861–1925), achieved worldwide fame as the originator of the Science of the Spirit known as anthroposophy. Out of his spiritual research he was able to provide indications for the renewal of many human activities including: medicine (anthroposophical medicine or anthroposophically-extended medicine), education (Waldorf education), religion (Christian Community), agriculture (biodynamics), special education (Camphill Movement), philosophy, economics, and art (eurythmy, speech, painting, drawing, and architecture).

3. Michaela Strauss, *Understanding Children's Drawings* (Rudolf Steiner Press, London, 1988), p. 49.

4. Kali Yuga, 3101–1899 BC, Hindu Age of Darkness.

5. Charles Wentinck, *The Human Figure* (Wynnewood, PA, 1996), p. 125.

6. Rudolf Steiner, *The Gospel of St. John* (Anthroposophic Press, New York, 1948), p. 130.

7. Wolff Husemann, *The Anthroposophical Approach to Medicine* (Anthroposophic Press, New York, 1982), ch. 2, p. 16.

8. Rudolf Steiner, *Karmic Relationships* (Rudolf Steiner Press, London, 1975), Vol. 8, Lecture 1, p. 13.

9. Genesis 1:27.

10. Op. cit., Steiner, *The Gospel of St. John*, Hamburg, Lecture 3, pp. 46–48.

11. Gerhard Reisch, from *Beings and Words of Wisdom*.

Illustrations

Introductory picture: *Mariah*, Monica Gold.

1   Drawing by a nine-year-old child.

Note: Illustrations 2 to 11 are from *The Human Figure in Art from Prehistoric Times to the Present Day* by Charles Wentinck (Livingston Publishing Company, Wynnewood, PA, 1970).

2   *Hunters*, Mesolithic wall painting, 15,000–10,000 BC, Castellon, Spain.

3   *Wounded Man and Rhinoceros*, assumed earliest Upper Palaeolithic 10,000 BC, Lascaux, Dordogne, France. The Cantabrian cave paintings range from 40,000 to 9000 BC.

4   *Ombra*, Etruscan, Etruscan Museum, Volterra, Italy.

5   *Elongated Figurine*, Etruscan, end of 5th c. BC, Umbria, Italy.

6   *Statue of Antinous as a God*, Roman, AD 140, National Museum, Naples, Italy.

7   *The Three Graces*, Raphael (1483–1520), Conde Museum, Chantilly, France.

8   *The Flayed*, Alessandro Allori (1535–1607), Louvre Museum, Paris, France.

9   *The Three Bathers*, Pierre-Auguste Renoir (1841–1919), Louvre Museum, Paris, France.

10   *Nude in the Forest*, Pablo Picasso (1881–1973), Hermitage Museum, St. Petersburg, Russia.

11   *Woman I*, Willem de Kooning (1904–1997), Museum of Modern Art, New York.

12   *Self-Portrait*, Joan Miró (1893–1983), Catalan painter, Spain (Roland Penrose, Thames and Hudson, London, 1970), Sra Pilar Juncosa de Miró, Palma de Mallorca. Photo: Courtesy, Gallerie Maeght.

13–17 Drawings by young children.

2. The Little Golden Box

Endnotes

1. Rudolf Steiner, *Background to the Gospel of St. Mark* (Rudolf Steiner Press, London, 1968), Lecture 4, p. 65.

2. Rudolf Steiner, *Angels, Selected Lectures: Spiritual Hierarchies as Cosmic Reality* (Rudolf Steiner Press, Forest Row, England, 2001), p. 137.

3. Rudolf Steiner, *Occult Science and Occult Development* (Rudolf Steiner Press, London, 1966), GA 152, p. 13. "The chief characteristic of ordinary thinking is that each single act of thinking injures the nervous system, and above all, the brain; it destroys something in the brain. Every thought means that a minute process of destruction takes place in the cells of the brain. For this reason sleep is necessary for us, in order that this process of destruction may be made good; during sleep is restored what during the day was destroyed in our nervous system by thinking. Highest hierarchies take part in this process. We now endeavor to practice meditation by devoting ourselves to contemplation, for instance, of the saying: 'Wisdom lives in Light.' This idea cannot originate from sense-impressions because according to the external senses it is not so. ...In meditative thinking no process of destruction is evoked in our nervous system; this kind of thinking never causes sleepiness, however long it may be continued, as ordinary thinking may easily do." Here we are connecting with the world of the Angeloi.

4. Rudolf Meyer, *The Wisdom of Fairy Tales* (Floris Books, Cromwell Press, Wilts, England, 1988), ch. 1, p. 17.

5. Rudolf Steiner, *Reincarnation and Karma: Their Significance in Modern Culture* (Anthroposophical Publishing Company, London, 1960, or Anthroposophical Press, New York, 1992), Lecture 4, p. 58.

6. Rudolf Steiner, *Theosophy* (Rudolf Steiner Press, London, 1970), ch. 2, pp. 66–67. "The body is subject to the law of heredity; the soul is subject to its self-created fate. Using an ancient expression, one calls this fate, created by the man himself, his karma. And the spirit is under the law of re-embodiment, repeated earth-lives. ...One can accordingly express the relationship between spirit, soul and body in the following way as well: The spirit is immortal; birth and death reign over the body according to the laws of the physical world; the soul-life, which is subject to destiny, mediates the connection of both during an earthly life." On p. 66 he says, "The physical body is subject to the laws of heredity. The human spirit, on the contrary, has to incarnate over and over again, and its law consists in its bringing over the fruits of the former lives into the following ones. The soul lives in the present, but this life in the present is not independent of the previous lives because the incarnating spirit brings its destiny with it from its previous incarnations. This destiny determines life. What impressions the soul will be able to have, what wishes it will be able to have gratified, what sorrows and joys shall develop for it, with what men and women it shall come into contact—all this depends upon the nature of the actions in the past incarnations of the spirit."

7.   Rudolf Steiner, *Truth, Beauty and Goodness* (Rudolf Steiner Publishing Company, London, 1986), GA 220, a lecture given in Dornach, Jan. 19, 1923; available online through the Rudolf Steiner Archive: elibrarian@elib.com. "An intense feeling for beauty—as it was then conceived—existed in earlier ages. Nothing of the same kind is present in modern civilization. To have no sense of beauty is to disregard, to disown the etheric body. When the Greek approached his temple, or beheld within the temple the statue of the god, he was conscious of an inner glowing warmth, a kind of inner sunlight. It was as though forces streamed into his being and into his different organs. Gazing at the statue of the god, his whole heart cried out, 'Never do I feel the peripheral structure of my hands and fingers so vividly as when this statue stands there before me!' Inwardly warmed and irradiated— God-inspired—this did the Greek feel in the presence of beauty. And this was nothing else but an experience in the etheric body."

8.   Rudolf Steiner, *Theosophy of the Rosicrucian* (Rudolf Steiner Press, London, 1981), ch. 3, pp. 35–36. Here he speaks about the time after death, when the transformed etheric and astral combine with the causal body. "What may be called ether or life-substance dissipates in the cosmic ether, but a kind of essence remains, and this can never be lost to the human being through his further journeying. He bears this with him into all his future incarnations as a kind of extract from the life-tableau, even though he has no remembrance of it." See also: Rudolf Steiner's *Founding a Science of the Spirit* (Rudolf Steiner Press, London, 1999), chs. 1 and 2.

9.   Rudolf Steiner, *The Gospel of St. Luke* (Rudolf Steiner Press, London, 1988), Lectures 2, 3, and 9: "Teachings of the Buddha—Compassion and Love."

10.   Rudolf Steiner, *Christianity as a Mystical Fact* (Anthroposophic Press, New York, 1947), Lecture 8, p. 137.

11.   Rudolf Steiner, *Karmic Relationships: Volume 1* (Rudolf Steiner Press, London, 1972), Lecture 1, p. 11. "I now wish to begin to speak to you of the laws and conditions of human destiny, which as you know, it has become customary to describe as karma. Karma, however, cannot be seen clearly unless we are prepared to learn to know the different kinds of universal law and universal activity."

12.   Rudolf Steiner, *The Work of the Angels in Man's Astral Body* (Rudolf Steiner Press, London, 1972), p. 20.

Illustrations

18   *Pharaoh Chephren with the Horus Falcon*, ca. 2700 BC, Egypt. Side view detail, Gottfried Richter, *Art and Human Consciousness* (SteinerBooks, Anthroposophic Press, Great Barrington, MA, 1985).

19, 20 *The Miracle of San Diego*, called *The Angels' Kitchen* (1646), Bartolomé Esteban Murillo (1617–1682). (The Masters, No. 30, Knowledge Publications, Purnell and Sons Ltd., Paulton/Bristol, England, 1966), Plates II, III.

21   *Angel*, Duccio di Buoninsegna (1255/60–1318/19). (The Masters, No. 11, Knowledge Publications, Purnell and Sons Ltd., Paulton/Bristol, England, 1966).

22   *Hestia, Dione, and Aphrodite Together with Other Gods*, ca. 470 BC, Parthenon, Greece. (Verlag Urachhaus, Stuttgart, 1976, Johannes M. Meyer GmbH & Co.).

23   *The Death of Niobide*, ca. 460 BC. Thermen Museum.

24   *The Birth of Aphrodite* (from Ludovisi throne), ca. 470 BC, Greek (Verlag Urachhaus, Stuttgart 1976, Johannes M. Meyer GmbH & Co.).

25   *Tombstone of Princess Sophia Volkonskaya* (1792–1862), Ivan Martos (Aurora Art Publishers, Leningrad, 1983).

26   *The Lord God Writing the Law*, William Blake (1757–1827), in *William Blake* by Kaethe Wolf-Gumpold (Rudolf Steiner Press, London, 1969, and Garden City Press Ltd., Letchworth, Herts).

3. The Firebird

Endnotes

1. William Wordsworth (1770–1850), "Ode: Intimations of Immortality from Recollections of Early Childhood" (1804).

2. *The Firebird*, illustrations by Ludek Manasek (J.M. Dent Sons Ltd., a Division of the Orion Publ. Group, London, 1969).

3. Rudolf Steiner, *Earthly Death and Cosmic Life* (Rudolf Steiner Press, London, 1964), p. 56.

4. Rudolf Steiner, *From Jesus to Christ* (Rudolf Steiner Press, Forest Row, UK, 2005), p. 16.

5. Dionysius the Areopagite, *Celestial Hierarchies*. Dionysius the Areopagite was a first-century Athenian who was converted to Christianity by St. Paul. He became the first bishop of Athens. His teaching was transferred by word of mouth to many generations of esoteric pupils. Each pupil took the name of Dionysius. In the fifth century, the last Dionysius wrote down his teachings into a book, *Celestial Hierarchy, Ecclesiastical Hierarchy, Concerning the Names of God, Mystical Divinity, and Ten Epistles* (Collier's Encyclopedia, New York, 1959).

6. Rudolf Steiner, *Universe, Earth and Man* (Rudolf Steiner Publishing Co., London, 1955), chs. 4, 5, p. 64.

7. Rudolf Steiner, *How to Know Higher Worlds* (Anthroposophical Press, Great Barrington, MA, 2002), p. 149. "The gifts that the student of the inner path receives by virtue of achieving this stage of development are these: insight into the higher self and into the doctrine of the embodiment or incarnation of this higher self in a lower-self; insight into the law by which life in the physical world is regulated according to spiritual relationships—the law of karma; and finally, insight into the existence of the great initiates." See also: Rudolf Steiner, *Theosophy* (Anthroposophic Press, New York, 1971), chs. 1, 2.

8. Rudolf Steiner, *Macrocosm and Microcosm* (Rudolf Steiner Press, London, 1968).

9. Rudolf Steiner, *Man in the Light of Occultism, Theosophy and Philosophy* (Spiritual Science Library, New York, 1989), chs. 5, 6. See also: Rudolf Steiner, *The Spiritual Hierarchies and Their Reflection in the Physical World* (Anthroposophic Press, New York, 1970).

10. Rudolf Steiner, *The Spiritual Hierarchies and Their Reflection in the Physical World* (Anthroposophic Press, New York, 1970), ch. 10, p. 139.

11. Rudolf Steiner, *The Festivals and Their Meaning: Ascension and Pentecost* (Rudolf Steiner Press, London, 1981), p. 250.

12. Lionel Stebbing, *The Secrets of Numbers* (New Knowledge Books, East Grinstead, UK, 1977), pp. 3, 4, 53.

13. Friedrich Husemann and Otto Wolff, eds., *The Anthroposophical Approach to Medicine* (Anthroposophic Press, Spring Valley, New York, 1982), ch. 3, p. 61.

14. Ellen E. Chaffee and Esther M. Greisheimer, *Basic Physiology and Anatomy* (J.B. Lippincott Company, Philadelphia, Montreal, 1964).

15. Ants have been living on the Earth for more than 100 million years and can be found almost anywhere on the planet. There are 20,000 different species. They have been called the Earth's most successful species. This social insect lives in colonies and builds a variety of homes.

16. Alfred Heidenreich, *The Catacombs* (The Christian Community Press, London, 1962), p. 23. "In designating Christ by the picture of the Fish, the principle of progress as the necessary enemy of all stagnation and reaction was expressed."

17. *Book of Tobit*. The text is apocryphal to the Protestant, canonical to the Catholic, and external to the Hebraic traditions. Taken from *The Occult in Art*, Fred Gettings (Rizzoli International Publications Inc., New York), p. 62.

18. Padraic Colum, *The Children of Odin* (The MacMillan Company, New York, 1948). The ravens are a powerful image in Nordic mythology: "Two ravens had Odin All-Father; Hugin and Munin were their names; they flew through all the worlds every day, and, coming back to Asgard, they would light on Odin's shoulders and tell him of all the things they had seen and heard in the world." See Walter Johannes Stein's *Weltgeschichte im Lichte des Heiligen Gral, Das Neunte Jahrhundert* (J.Ch. Mellinger Verlag, Stuttgart, 1966), p. 131. In *World History in the Light of the Holy Grail: The Ninth Century*, Basilius Valentinus (15th century Benedictine monk and alchemist) describes the black raven as a first grade of initiation, a time when a student on the spiritual path still walks in the dark and knows the spirit light only through study.

19. The magic flute is for Mozart the imagination of the will. When Tamino plays it, he is able to pass the tests set for him by Zarastro. Tamino is asked to go through fire, which has a purifying effect.

20. Baked from flour and stuffed with a variety of fillings, pirozhkis are a national specialty in Russia.

21. Rudolf Steiner, *Occult Science and Occult Development* (Rudolf Steiner Press, London, 1966), p. 2, as well as *How to Know Higher Worlds* (Rudolf Steiner Press, London, 1969). Spiritual Science distinguishes between intellectual and imaginative thinking. It shows us how living thoughts instead of dry intellectual ones can fill the mind. Spiritual, "light-filled" thinking includes prayer and meditation, and the result of such an activity when pursued long enough is imaginative thinking.

22. Rudolf Steiner, *Occult Physiology* (Rudolf Steiner Press, London, 1983), pp. 136–137.

23. Carl E. Schmoeger, *The Life of Anne Catherine Emmerich* (TAN Books and Publishers Inc., Rockford, IL, 1968). "The nun, Anne Catharine Emmerich was four years old when she decided that she wanted to pray at night and not sleep. She fastened a knotted belt around her waist, lay on the cold ground, and prayed for three hours at this early age. When she was older, she no longer slept but worked spiritually day and night. Her will was used only in the service of others by praying and taking their suffering on to her shoulders. This is an example of someone who is totally selfless."

24. Rudolf Steiner, *Universe, Earth and Man* (Rudolf Steiner Publishing Co., London, 1955), See App. No. 6, p. 64. Also: Rudolf Steiner, *The Spiritual Hierarchies and Their Reflection in the Physical World* (Anthroposophic Press, New York, 1970), ch. 10.

Illustrations

27 *Virgin and Child* detail from the *Isenheim Altarpiece,* 1515, Matthias Grünewald (The Masters, No. 83, Knowledge Publications, Purnell and Sons Ltd., Paulton/Bristol, England, 1967).

28 *La Ronde des Élus*, Fra Angelico, 15th c. (The Masters, No. 78, Museo di San Marco, Firenze. Editions Abbaye of en calcat, 81110 Courgne [Tarn] Drager, Imp. Procede 301).

29 *Seraphim*, Byzantine, Abbey Church, Hurez, Romania. RU Artcard: No. 2609 (Raphael Verlag, Stockhornstrasse 5, CH-3063 Ittingen).

30 *Anatomical Man* from *Les Très Riches Heures du Duc de Berry,* 15th c. manuscript; text by Edmond Pognon, Musée Condé, Chantilly, France (Photos: Bibliothèque Nationale, Paris. Printed in Spain).

31 *Zodiacal Man*, from a 16th c. manuscript, *The Guild Book of the Barber: Surgeons of York*, British Museum, London. Fred Gettings, *The Occult in Art* (Rizzoli International Publications Inc., New York, 1978), Illustration 41, p. 49.

32–34 Illustrations by seven- to nine-year-old children showing the nine-year-old change.

35 *Fish and Anchor*, early Christian, Domitilla Catacombs, in *Die Katakomben* by Emil Bock and Robert Goebel (Verlag Urachhaus, Stuttgart, 1961).

36 *Tobias and the Angel* ca. 1480, Andrea del Verrocchio (National Gallery, London), in Fred Gettings, *The Occult in Art* (Rizzoli International Publications Inc., New York, 1978), Illustration 77, p. 62.

37 *Mother of God, praying in the Orans position*, mosaic, Sophia Cathedral, Kiev (*Kirchen und Kloester im alten Russland,* Verlag Anton Schroll & Co., Vienna and Munich, 1982). One can find illustrations of departed souls in the Orans position in the Catacombs in Rome.

38 *The Temptation of St. Anthony* from the *Isenheim Altarpiece* (1515), Matthias Grünewald, in Georg Scheja, *The Isenheim Altar* (Du Mont's Neue Kunst-Reihe, Verlag M. Du Mont Schauberg, Cologne, 1969).

39 The crucifix which spoke to St. Francis at San Damiano, 12th c., Basilica di Santa Chiara, Assisi, Italy (from a replica). In 1206 as St. Francis of Assisi was passing by the San Damiano Church (Chiesa di S. Chiara), which was almost in ruins, he was moved by the Spirit to enter and pray before the cross of San Damiano. A voice coming from the cross told him three times: "Francis, go and repair My house which you can see is falling into ruin." It changed his life.

4. The Fisher-Prince with the Silver Apple

Endnotes

1.   Isabel Wyatt, *The Book of Fairy Princes* (Floris Books, Edinburgh, 2000).

2.   A.C. Harwood, T*he Way of a Child* (Anthroposophic Press, Hudson, NY), ch. 1, pp. 15–16.

3.   Rudolf Steiner, *Spiritual Beings in the Heavenly Bodies and in the Kingdoms of Nature* (Anthroposophic Press, Hudson, NY, 1992), Lecture 9, p. 162: "We said that human beings have the four principles of their being active on the physical plane: the physical body, etheric body, astral body, and I. Then we drew attention to the fact that, in the animal three principles are active on the physical plane—the physical, etheric and astral bodies—while the group Ego is on the astral plane."

4.   Rudolf Steiner, *The Interpretation of Fairy Tales* (Rudolf Steiner Publishing Co, Anthroposophic Press, New York, 1929), pp. 9, 17, 19.

5.   Ibid., pp. 17, 31. "Nowadays, however, we can very seldom find anyone who can relate things from a genuine source; and it will be said of fairy tale experiences—They happened once upon a time and if they are not dead, these fairy tale experiences still live."

6.   Rudolf Meyer, *The Wisdom in Fairy Tales* (Floris Books, Edinburgh, 1997).

7.   Rudolf Steiner, *Karmic Relationships*, Volume 5 (Rudolf Steiner Press, London, 1997), Lecture 2, pp. 21, 22.

8.   Rudolf Steiner, *The Temple Legend* (Rudolf Steiner Press, London, 1985), ch. 2. The first stream is represented in the Temple Legend by Abel; the second is represented by Cain. Their stories can be read in the Old Testament.

9.   Op. cit., Steiner, *Spiritual Beings in Heavenly Bodies and in the Kingdom of Nature*, ch. 10, p. 196: "Silver arose through etheric streams, which the spirits of wisdom sent to the earth from the moon in order to bring the earth back into balance."

10. Audrey E. McAllen, *Sleep: An Unobserved Element in Education* (Hawthorn Press, Stroud, UK, 1986), ch. 2, "The Threefold Experience of Sleep."

11. John 1:12.

12. Rudolf Steiner, *The Spiritual Hierarchies and Their Reflection in the Physical World* (Anthroposophic Press, New York, 1970), Lecture 10, pp. 137–138: "The Christ is a God who does not act in such a way that His impulses have necessarily to be followed; one follows Him out of understanding and only out of freedom. He is, therefore, the God who never seeks to hinder the free development in one or other direction. In the deepest sense of the word Christ could say, 'You will know the Truth and the Truth will make you free.' The beings of the next hierarchy, the Luciferic beings who had the possibility of doing evil, will be released again through the power of man." Also, "Man has to fulfill a completely new mission in the world. …It belongs to the lofty mission of man to bring freedom into the

world, and together with freedom, what is called love. If love is to enter our cosmos, it can happen only through freedom."

13. *Rudolf Steiner*, edited and introduced by Christopher Bamford (SteinerBooks, Great Barrington, MA, 2004), p. 143.

14. Rudolf Steiner, *Twelve Moods* (Mercury Press, New York, 1984).

15. Op. cit., Steiner, *The Spiritual Hierarchies and Their Reflection in the Physical World*, Lecture 4, p. 49.

16. Ezekiel 1:10.

17. Revelation 4:6, 7–14.

18. Rudolf Steiner, *Man in the Light of Occultism, Theosophy and Philosophy* (Spiritual Science Library, New York, 1989).

19. Rudolf Steiner, *The Gospel of Saint John Cassel* (Anthroposophic Press, New York, 1948), Lecture 8, p. 118: "Those who saw the spiritual counterparts as Bull spirits bore testimony to the spiritual world by introducing a Bull worship, which led on the one hand to the Apis Bull worship in Egypt, and on the other, to the worship of the Persian Mithras Bull; for everything we find in the way of outer cult usages among the different peoples derived from the initiation rites."

20. Rudolf Steiner, *Earthly Death and Cosmic Life* (Rudolf Steiner Press, London, 1964), Lecture 3, p. 56.

21. Rudolf Steiner, *Wonders of the World, Ordeals of the Soul, Revelations of the Spirit* (Rudolf Steiner Press, London, 1963), ch. 9, p. 158. A further explanation on the same page: "If one allows such a sphinx, made up of a lion-form and a bull-form, together with the wings of a bird, to work upon the clairvoyant vision, and if one completes it by adding the human Phantom (God-given blueprint of man's physical body) which underlies it, if one weaves these elements together, then the human form as we have it today comes into being before us."

22. Beredene Jocelyn, *What Difference Did the Deed of Christ Make?* (Rudolf Steiner Information Centre, New York, 1968), p. 10.

23. Rudolf Steiner, *The Four Seasons and the Archangels* (Rudolf Steiner Press, London, 1968), Lecture 1: "The Michael Imagination," p. 19.

24. Rudolf Steiner, *An Occult Physiology*, "Blood as Manifestation and Instrument of the Human Ego" (Rudolf Steiner Publishing Co., London, 1951), ch. 6, p. 128.

25. Revelation 6:4–8.

26. John 4:10.

27. John 15:1.

28. John 6:35.

29. Genesis 9:20.

30. Rudolf Steiner, *The Fairy Tale of the Green Snake and the Beautiful Lily* by Johann Wolfgang von Goethe (SteinerBooks, New York, 1979), p. 61. Rudolf Steiner, *The Character of Goethe's Spirit* (Garber Communications, New York, 1991): "What separates man from 'free personality' is that these three [gold, silver and copper] work in his soul as a mixture; he will achieve free personality in the measure in which he can receive in full consciousness the gift of these three with their own special quality, each of them separately, and unite them himself in free, conscious activity within his soul. Only then what previously enslaved him collapses into itself—the chaotic mixture of the gifts of the will, the feeling and the power of knowledge."

Illustrations

40   *The Hero Gilgamesh*, Assyrian, 8th c. BC. Dur-Sharrukin, Khorsabad. Louvre Museum, Paris. Charles Wentinck, *The Human Figure*, p. 66, Plate 24 (Livingston Publishing Co, Wynnewood, PA, 1909).

41   *Lamassu guardian figure* [in background L., relief of the Hero Gilgamesh], from the Palace of Sargon II at Dur-Sharrukin (modern Khorsabad), ca. 713–706 BC. Louvre Museum, Paris, Courtesy Allan T. Kohl/Art Images for College Teaching (AICT).

42   *The Vision of Ezekiel*, Raphael (1483–1520) (Instituto Geografico de Agostini, Novara. Printed in Italy, 1959), Plate N.11.

43   *The Son of Man*, 12th c. Chartres Cathedral, Tympanum of the Royal Portal, in Gottfried Richter, *Chartres* (Verlag Urachhaus Johannes M Mayer GmbH & Co., Stuttgart, 1976), Plate 17, p. 56.

44–47 *The Book of Kells*, ca. AD 800, Plates 19, 49, 59 and 91, reproductions from the manuscript in Trinity College, Dublin (Thames and Hudson, London, 1974).

48   *The Great Sphinx*, Giza, Egypt, 2530 BC, in Frederick Hartt, *Art: A History of Painting, Sculpture and Architecture* (Harry N. Abrams, Inc., New York, 1976), Plate 62, p. 63.

49   *The Ecstasy of St. Cecilia*, ca. 1516, Raphael. Gemaeldegalerie, Berlin, in *One Hundred Saints*, (A Bulfinch Press Book, Little, Brown and Company, Boston, 2002), p. 67.

50   Drawing by a ten-year-old child.

51   *The Risen Christ*, Graduale from St. Gallen, 11th c. Stiftsbibliothek, St. Gallen (ms 376. Beuroner Kunstverlag D 7792), Beuron, postcard.

52   Drawing by an eleven-year-old child.

5. The Crystal Ball and the Silver Saucer

Endnotes

1. Rudolf Steiner, *The Spiritual Hierarchies and Their Reflection in the Physical World* (Anthroposophic Press, New York, 1970), Lecture 10, p. 139.

2. Rudolf Steiner, *The Interpretation of Fairy Tales* (Anthroposophic Press, New York, 1943), p. 11: "The first thing to which we must closely adhere when relating fairy tales, legends or myths is that we must certainly know more than we are able to say, indeed, a great deal more; and secondly, we should be willing to draw the sources of our explanation from anthroposophical wisdom: that is to say, we must not introduce into the fairy tales just anything that may occur to us, but must be willing to recognize anthroposophical wisdom as such, and then try and permeate the fairy tales therewith."

3. Alice Raphael, *Goethe and the Philosopher's Stone* [Faust 1], (Routledge & Kegan Paul, London, 1965), p. 63.

4. *The New Testament*, a modern rendering by Jon Madsen (Floris Books, Edinburgh, 2006), p. 66. See also: Mark 9:37 and 10:14.

5. Rudolf Steiner, *True and False Paths in Spiritual Investigation* (Rudolf Steiner Press, London/ Anthroposophic Press, New York, 1985).

6. Rudolf Steiner, *The Philosophy of Freedom: The Basis for a Modern World Conception* (Rudolf Steiner Press, London, 1964), and *How to Know Higher Worlds* (Anthroposophic Press, Great Barrington, MA, 2002).

7. Rudolf Steiner, *The Way of Initiation* (The Occult Publishing Company, Chicago, 1909), p. 74.

8. Rudolf Steiner, *Angels*, selected lectures (Rudolf Steiner Press, London 1996), Lecture given in Oslo, 7 June 1910, Arnheim 1924, p.101. Several archangels, leaders of the planets, have been given the task of guiding different civilizations. The most commonly known are the Archangels Michael, Raphael and Gabriel, along with Oriphiel, Anael, Zachariel and Samael. Sun = Michael 601–247 BC, Saturn = Oriphiel 247 BC–AD 150, Venus = Anael 1 50–500 AD, Jupiter = Zachariel 500–850 AD, Mercury = Raphael 850–1190 AD, Mars = Samael 1190–1510 AD, Moon = Gabriel 1510–1879 AD, Michael 1879–.

9. Irmgard and Reinhart Engelen, *Rudolf Steiner über Russland* (Dornach, Switzerland: Rudolf Steiner Verlag, Auszüge aus dem Gesamtwerk. Internationale Vereinigung der Waldorfkindergarten, Stuttgart, 1975), Lecture GA 174B Stuttgart 12.3.16.

10. Genesis 1:2: "And the Spirit of God moved over the face of the waters."

11. Theodor Schwenk, *Sensitive Chaos: The Creation of Flowing Forms in Water and Air* (Rudolf Steiner Press, Forest Row, UK, 2004), pp. 49–50: "The form of the vortex, with its quality of creating a connection with the surrounding world, appears in the horns of many animals. Horns may often be regarded as delicate sense organs that guide the animal."

12. Michael Jones, *Nuclear Energy: A Spiritual Perspective* (Floris Books, Edinburgh, 1983), pp. 65–66: "The ether stream from the Sun enters earth directly in the substance gold, and indirectly in the other earthly substances which have passed through the planetary interweaving. Homoeopathic gold works medically on the bloodstream, the physical basis for the ego in man." Strengthening of the ego goes into the future—"silver tends to dull consciousness and is used in the regeneration of the reproductive. …Gold and silver represent a polarity in the etheric world…," and "a new etheric current was set up from the moon, and working in opposition to the Sun currents gave rise to the metal silver on earth, a sign of the restoring of equilibrium to the life of nature."

13. Oskar Daehnert, *Johann Wolfgang von Goethe*, Volume 1 (Verlag Schlueter & Ulbrich, Leipzig, 1925), from "The Spirit Song over the Waters," p. 58, translated by Monica Gold.

14. Op. cit., Engelen. See also Lecture GA 173, Dornach 9.12.16 and Lecture GA 157, Berlin, 22.6.15.

15. John 11:25.

16. John 4:14.

17. Corinne Heline, *Color and Music in the New Age* (De Vorss & Company Publishers, Marina del Ray, CA, 1985).

18. Rudolf Steiner, *Das Wesen der Farben [The Essence of the Colors]* (Rudolf Steiner Verlag, Dornach, 1973), p. 35.

19. Ibid., p. 51.

20. Ibid., p. 44.

21. Ram-headed sphinxes line the processional avenue before the Temple of Amun-Re at Karnak. A symbol of fertility, the ram also projects power. The sphinx, a creature of parts, was usually a lion with a man's head. In this version, the sphinx honors Amun, the king of gods, with its head. The rest of the body becomes "the celestial lion throne of Re."

22. True pyramids (at least the larger ones), as opposed to step pyramids in Egypt, were topped by a special stone called a *pyramidion* (or sometimes a capstone), which was itself a miniature pyramid. It brought the pyramid structure to a point at the same angle and the same proportions as the main body. Actually, the ancient Egyptian word for the pyramidion, which could also sit atop the apex of an obelisk, was *benbenet*, named for the sacred Ben-ben stone kept in the temple of Heliopolis, the oldest center of the sun cult in Egypt.

23. Gottfried Richter, *Art and Human Consciousness* (Anthroposophic Press, Great Barrington, MA, 1985), p. 12.

24. Ibid., p. 15.

25. Rudolf Steiner, *From Symptom to Reality in Modern History* (Rudolf Steiner Press, London, 1976), Lecture 8. See also: GA 185, Dornach 2.11.18.

26. Ibid., p. 188: "We mean by this that a territory has been set apart in the East of Europe where men lived who were directly united with the Christ impulse. The Christ is ever present as an inner aura impregnating the thinking and feeling of these people."

27. Victor Bott, *Anthroposophical Medicine: An Extension of the Art of Healing* (Rudolf Steiner Press, London, 1982). This book gives an idea of the lecture content that was given in Russia.

28. Op. cit., Steiner, *From Symptom to Reality in Modern History*, Lecture 8, p. 190.

29. Rudolf Steiner, "Die Geistigen Hintergruende des Ersten Weltkrieges," GA 174B, Stuttgart, 12.3.16. Also see: Irmgard and Reinhart Engelen, *Rudolf Steiner über Russland* (Dornach, Switzerland: Rudolf Steiner Verlag, Auszuege aus dem Gesamtwerk. Internationale Vereinigung der Waldorfkindergarten, Stuttgart, 1975), p. 3.

30. *Collier's Encyclopedia*, Volume 5, (Collier & Son Corporation, New York, 1959): A formal letter written on behalf of The Christian Community urging Christians, who had been rebelling against church authority, to be submissive and obedient. Tradition attributes it to Clement, allegedly one of the first bishops of Rome, ca. AD 96.

31. Op. cit., Steiner, *Spiritual Hierarchies and Their Reflection in the Spiritual World*, p. 128.

32. Op. cit., Engelen, Lecture GA 174B, Stuttgart, 12.3.16.

Illustrations

53   Copy of *The Head of Christ* from *The Last Supper* (1495–1497). Imitator of Leonardo da Vinci, Brera Gallery, Milan. On behalf of the Italian Ministery of Artistic and Cultural Heritage.

54   *The Good and Evil Angels Struggling for Possession of a Child*, William Blake, 1757–1827, in Kaethe Wolf-Gumpold, *William Blake: Painter, Poet, Visionary* (Rudolf Steiner Press, London, 1969).

55–57 *Sensitive Chaos: The Creation of Flowing Forms in Water and Air*, Theodor Schwenk (Rudolf Steiner Press, London 1965), Plates 33, 34, 41 and 42.

58   *The Christ*, 12th c. Basilique de la Madeleine. Le Christ du Tympare Central, Narthex, 89450 Vezelay. Imp. Traditions Monastiques F. 211 50 Flavigny 80.96.22.31, Cliché Magasin du Pelarin Nar/tym GC.

59   *The Threefold Man*, (*Der dreigliedrige Mensch*), 1923. Rudolf Steiner (1861–1925). Postcard, Dornach 2002. Aus der Reihe der Schulungsskizzen für Maler, GA K 54.14 (Rudolf Steiner Nachlassverwaltung, Dornach, Schweiz, Rudolf Steiner Verlag, CH 4143 Dornach).

60   Processional Path with Sphinxes at the Temple at Luxor, Egypt, 400 BC, Frank Teichmann, *Der Mensch und sein Tempel, Egypt* (Urachhaus, Stuttgart, 1978).

61   Cathedral of the Birth of Mary, in the Kremlin, Russia, ca. AD 1225. Hubert Faensen (Verlag Anton Schroll & Co., Vienna and Munich, 1982).

62   Ibid., floor plan of the same cathedral.

63   Typical interior of an Eastern Orthodox church.

64   Cathedral and Cathedral Court, Ratzeburg, Germany, 8th c. Heinz-Dietrich Gross in *Die Blauen Bücher* (Hans Koester, Koenigstein, 1974).

65   Speyer Cathedral floor plan, ca. 1040, in *Art and Human Consciousness*, Gottfried Richter (SteinerBooks/Anthroposophic Press, Great Barrington, MA, 1985).

66   *Rout of the Rebel Angels*, William Blake (1757–1827) in *William Blake at the Huntington*, Robert Essick (Harry N. Abrams Inc., Publishers, San Marino, CA, 1994).

67   Ancient coat of arms of Novgorod, Russia. Maria Schindler, *Europe, a Cosmic Picture* (Horsham, Sussex, 1975).

68   *Man with Light*, 1962, Alexander Kharitinov, in *Unofficial Art in the Soviet Union*, Paul Sjeklocha and Igor Mead (University of California Press, Berkeley, CA, 1967).

6. Bashtchelik or True Steel

Endnotes

1. *Bashtchelik or True Steel*, a Serbian fairy tale from *The Key of the Kingdom*, collected by Elisabeth Gmeyner and Joyce Russell (Rudolf Steiner Press, London, 1966).

2. 1 Corinthians 13:13. See also lecture by Rudolf Steiner, "Faith, Love and Hope: The Third Revelation to Mankind," *Golden Blade* 194, Nurnberg, Dec. 2–3, 1911.

3. Rudolf Steiner, *The Interpretation of Fairy Tales* (Rudolf Steiner Publishing Co., Anthroposophic Press, New York, 1943).

4. Ibid., pp. 12–14.

5. 1 Samuel 17:1–58

6. Rudolf Steiner, *Universe, Earth and Man* (Rudolf Steiner Publishing Co., London, 1955), p. 154.

7. Rudolf Steiner, *The Spiritual Hierarchies and Their Reflection in the Physical World* (Anthroposophic Press, New York, 1970), p. 128.

8. Rudolf Steiner, *Egyptian Myths and Mysteries* (Anthroposophic Press, New York, 1971), p. 122.

9. Matthew 6:22–23.

10. Paul M. Allen, *Vladimir Soloviev: Russian Mystic* (Rudolf Steiner Publication, London, 1978), p. 13.

11. Victor Bott, *Anthroposophical Medicine* (Thorsons Publishers Inc., New York, 1984).

12. Op. cit., Steiner, *The Interpretation of Fairy Tales*, p. 21.

13. Rudolf Steiner, *The Influences of Lucifer and Ahriman* (Steiner Book Centre Inc., North Vancouver, 1976). Also: Rudolf Steiner, *The Balance in the World and Man: Lucifer and Ahriman* (Steiner Book Centre Inc., North Vancouver, 1977).

14. Galatians 2:20.

15. Rudolf Steiner, *Michaelmas and the Soul Forces of Man* (Anthroposophic Press, Spring Valley, NY, 1982), Lecture 1, p. 10. See also quote from Bernard Nesfield-Cookson, *Michael and the Two-Horned Beast* (London, 1988), ch. 1, p. 4.

16. Op cit., Steiner, *The Interpretation of Fairy Tales*, pp. 11, 17.

17. Rudolf Steiner, *Occult Physiology* (Rudolf Steiner Press, London, 1983), p. 137.

18. Rudolf Steiner, *Gospel of St. John Cassel* (Anthroposophic Press, New York, 1948), p. 206.

19. Rudolf Steiner, *Christianity as a Mystical Fact* (Anthroposophic Press, New York, 1947), Lecture 8, p. 141.

20. Rudolf Steiner, *Karma of Materialism* (Anthroposophic Press, Inc., London, 1985), ch. l, p. 91. See also Rudolf Steiner, *Christ and the Human Soul*.

21. Op. cit., Steiner, *Gospel of St. John*, Lecture 13, p. 223.

22. Judy Allen and Jeanne Griffiths, *The Book of the Dragon* (Orbis Publishing Ltd., London, 1979), p. 36.

23. Rudolf Steiner, *The Deed of the Christ and the Opposing Spiritual Powers* (Rudolf Steiner Press Inc., North Vancouver, 1976), 2nd edition, p. 18.

24. Matthew 3:11 and Luke 3:16: "John answered, saying unto them all, I indeed baptize you with water; but one mightier than I cometh, the latchet of whose shoes I am not worthy to unloose. He shall baptize you with the Holy Ghost and with fire."

25. Rudolf Steiner, *Macrocosm and Microcosm* (Rudolf Steiner Press, London, 1968), p. 73.

Illustrations

69   *The Kiss of Death*, Hans Baldung (1480–1545), in Gottfried Richter, *Art and Human Consciousness* (SteinerBooks/Anthroposophic Press, Great Barrington, MA, 1985), p. 199.

70   *The Dance of Death*, A. Koburger, 15th c., ibid.

71   *The Archangel Michael and Golgotha*, wallpainting in Holland, 11th c., in *Aus Michaels Wirken*, a collection of legends by Nora Stein von Baditz (J.Ch. Mellinger Verlag, Stuttgart, 1959).

72   *Saint Michael and the Dragon* from *Les Très Riches Heures du Duc de Berry*, illuminated manuscript, Mont St. Michel, France, 15th c. (Edmond Pognon, Bibliothèque Nationale, Productions Liber SA, and Editions Minerva SA Fribourg, Geneve, 1979).

73   *The Serpent of the Garden of Eden*, from *The Book of the Dragon*, Judy Allen and Jeanne Griffiths (Chartwell Books Inc., New Jersey, Orbis Publishing Limited, London, 1979), p. 15.

74   *Michael and the Serpent*, Monte Gargano, Italy, 10th c., in *Vergessene Kulturen im Monte Gargano [Forgotten Civilizations in Monte Gargano]* (Verlag Hilfswerk Elisabeth, Stuttgart, 1970).

75   *The Holy Archangel Michael*, Ambrogio Lorenzetti (1290–1348), in *Aus Michaels Wirken*, op. cit.

76   *The Dragon of Wantley*, England, in *The Book of the Dragon*, op. cit., p. 105.

77   *St. Michael Weighing the Souls, Surrounded by Trumpeting Angels*, ca. 1445–1450, by Rogier van der Weyden (1399/1400–1464), in *Aus Michaels Wirken*, op. cit.

78   The interlocking yin yang symbol pursued by two dragons, mother of pearl inlay on a late 18th c. piece of furniture from Vietnam, in *The Book of the Dragon*, op. cit.

79   Imperial dragon on a Mandarin robe, Ch'ing Dynasty, China, in *The Book of the Dragon*, op. cit., p. 42.

80   *Representative of Man*, 1922, Rudolf Steiner. Sculpture in Dornach, Switzerland (Rudolf Steiner Press, 1975, Letchworth, Herts., SG6 1JS).

81   *St. Michael the Archangel*, ca. 1663, Luca Giordano. Gemäldegalerie, Berlin, in *One Hundred Saints* (A Bulfinch Press Book, Little, Brown & Company, Boston, 1993).

82   *Praying Madonna*, ca. 1200, Sinai, Monastery of St. Catherine, in *Icons in Sinai, Greece and Jugoslavia*, K. Weitzmann, M. Chatzidakis and S. Radojcic (Manfred Pawlak Verlagsgesellschaft mbH. Herrsching, 1980, German edition).

83   *The Trinity*, a 15th c. painting found in St. Peter's Church, Basel, Switzerland.